*From the **Eyes** of a **Child** to the Soul of a **Man**: A **Journey** along the **Highway** of **Life***

Chester (Chuck) Fuller, Ph.D.

Publishing Services: Stanton Publishing House

Library of Congress Registration Number: 2019934337

ISBN-13:9781987031997 (BARNES & NOBLES HARDBACK)

ISBN-13:9781987032017 (BARNES & NOBLES PAPERBACK)

ISBN-13:9781795448628 (KDP AMAZON)

Printed in the United States of America

Cover & Interior Design by Stanton Publishing House

The Author

Dr. Chester (Chuck) Fuller is a retired social scientist, researcher, and educator, having K-12 and university experience. Dr. Fuller 's professional experience began with the "Great Society," the War on Poverty Program in Detroit during the mid-ninth teenage in the sixties, following three years of service with the United States Marine Corps. Dr. Fuller earned degrees in Psychology (B.A.), Clinical Psychology (M.A.), and his Ph.D. in Counseling Psychology. His former positions include working as Research Associate with several major universities, Adjunct Professor/Site.

Administrator, Central Michigan University (Atlanta Campus), President of the Association of Black Psychologist (Atlanta Chapter), President and Founder of Urban Specialist Consolidated.

Dedicated to

My mother and father

My eleven sisters and brothers

My daughter (Lisa) and son (Eric)

My three granddaughters: (Aundrea, Erica, Macy)

And to Jean, the mother of our children and the essence

of my soul.

Table of Contents

Preface

Why do I write this book? Do I write this book because I want to? No, because that would be selfish of me and would be seeing life through the eyes of a child. Then, do I write this book because I can? No, because that would be putting my arrogance, adult self on display. Do I write this book because I must? Yes, my journey, as seen through the eyes of a child, to the soul of a man, dictates that I must. I write this book for my mother, as she says...” Chest, bless your soul,” and my father, as he says “boy…” I write it for my two children and my three granddaughters. I write it for my 11 brothers and sisters and their children’s, children. But, above all, I write this book for and because of Jean, my wife, my love, the mother of our children, and the essence of my soul. She would expect no less.

Introduction

Both the essence and purpose of this book are to examine the path taken by one individual, as he journeys from childhood to adulthood, and encounters the various challenges posed by life itself. The situations that he faced are in many instances, similar, if not identical to those faced by us all. Part of the intent here is to observe and examine how his perceptions and actions are impacted by the fact that he is in the transition from seeing the world through the eyes of a child to seeing the world through the eyes of an adult, all of which is juxtaposed with the forming of his soul. In the process of maturing, and dealing with the vicissitudes associated with living, he learns some of "life's lessons." Each life lesson, whether adopted or ignored, helps to form and shape his soul.

Each of the chapters included in this book contains "Life's Lesson Learned" from the author's life journey. Each of the life lessons learned is written in *italics*, and with a couple of exceptions, each of the lessons is original. A separate section at the end of the book provides a summary of all the author's life lessons learned, as well as a reflection of his soul.

There have been, throughout the history of mankind, many attempts to define exactly what constitutes the soul, and where it resides, but still, the search continues. The biblical perspective of Human Soul, states that "the soul is a part of a person that is not physical." The scriptures further accentuate the importance of the soul in [Matthew 16:26], ***"Jesus asks what good is it for a man to gain the whole world but lose his soul."[1]*** Following a similar trend of thought, the philosophical perspective advances the belief that "the soul is that which gives the body life but is separate from the body."

According to the Merriam-Webster Dictionary: *"The soul is the immaterial essence, animating principle, or actuating cause of an individual life."* It quickly becomes obvious, to those who care, that all the attempts to define the soul contain some similarities, but morphs toward becoming an exercise in "mystical redundancy." Still, the search is the both, necessary and required. As it has often been stated, "it is the journey, not the destination that is important." For purposes of this writing, think of the soul as what remains in an individual after all the exaggerations, denials, superficialities, and untruths have been removed, all that remains is the truth, or simply stated, the soul.

It must be stated, however, that what resides in the soul, may not be what is evident or exhibited from the soul of the individual. In short, the fact that an individual may profess to, or have a "good heart," does not ensure that the person will do "good-hearted" acts. Yes, I believe it to be true that every person has a soul; still, it would be illogical to believe that "All have good Souls."

As human beings, we all start and end at the same place… we are born, and we die. What happens between being born and dying constitutes the essence of our lives, namely, "life's journey. "The highway that our life journey travels contain many signs that provide us with valuable information to guide us on our journey. The signs tell us our location, the direction that we are traveling, the maximum speed that we can travel, and any potential hazard or detour we might encounter on life's highway. As children, we experience or see life through the eyes of a child. As we mature and travel further along life's highway, we begin to better understand what the signs along our journey are telling us. We still, however, make choices regarding whether we pay attention to the signs or ignore them. Either way, the signs have an impact upon us, albeit, the impact often resides in the subconscious, dormant, but not dead. Through it all, one must consider other options in defining the soul. This book is based, in part, upon the assertion that the soul is like a "Tabula rasa," or a blank slate. In effect, advancing the belief that the soul begins as an empty vessel, and filled throughout life's journey with experiences that the soul has no control over. The other side of the debate holds that the soul acts upon the journey by selecting certain life experiences to accept or reject, implying that the soul's structure is already formed and only accepts those life experiences that serve to fulfill its' mission or destiny. This entire debate is like the "nature versus nurture" debate pertaining to how an individual's personality is formed.

The soul is not static; it is a dynamic, living entity that not only requires continuous substance but periodic maintenance as well. To fully understand what constitutes substance for the soul, one must consider the belief that the soul reviews all of life's experiences, on both a conscious and subconscious levels before deciding to accept or reject the experiences as fulfilling the soul's structure or destiny. Therefore, the substance for the soul is the sum-total of life's experiences while traveling life's highway. Although the term "soul food" is sometimes used as an ethnic jargon to describe a particular food-type, that feeds the soul, the term represents a "bridge too far" to equate it to the meaning of soul for our purposes. However, I must add that everyone's soul has different forms of soul-substance that it responds to. Personally, when one of my children calls me "daddy or dad." I can't help but feel a surge in my soul, being a parent means that much and more to both my soul and me. The maintenance of the soul involves periodic assessments relative to the degree to which the soul is operating as expected, and at the expected level of proficiency. For example, do the individual's beliefs and actions reflect the "true" essence of the soul?

Most of us have had the experience of "feeling that something is just not right," prior to taking a stance or deciding. That is an example of the soul performing its own, internal assessment. This is the soul's way of telling us that, it is doing its job. There are or will be other times when the individual must do his or her own soul maintenance assessment by reflecting on recent personal actions or responses to situations. The individual typically feels a need for a soul assessment or maintenance when he or she senses a disconnection between something he feels or knows. In effect, the individual is experiencing "cognitive dissonance."

Although this book is written in a "Quasi-Autobiographical" style, in truth, the process of viewing life through a series of stages and significant incidents that happened at each stage, is mentally clarifying for us all. The book is also philosophical and reflective for the expressed purpose of allowing us to look backward, as well as forwards at our individual life-journey, from a three-dimensional perspective. It is often difficult or impossible to see ourselves from a broad, external view. This, in part, explains why all of us like to see pictures of ourselves, especially with others. We view that kind of pictures as though we're looking at individuals that we have never seen before. The smile that comes to our faces at that moment, serves as both an affirmation of self and of our existence.

This book provides glimpses into one person's life's-journey, while selectively presenting various occurrences and incidents that significantly impacted or changed life's journey's direction, or at the very minimum, impacted how this one person perceived something. The "something" that is impacted or changed may have been major or totally insignificant.

We have often heard the expression: "From the mouths of babes." One summer day, while playing in the back yard with my two granddaughters, Macy, the youngest, age six, stopped playing and asked me a question: Granddad, "why do you have gray hair and wrinkled hands?" Erica, her older sister of eight, and in an "older" sister's voice, offered her younger sister an explanation: "Macy, you are born, you get old, and then you die, let's play." While the answer that Erica gave to Macy, was a sufficient enough answer to satisfy her inquiry, it also helped to bring a harsh, yet, true reality to mind for me, namely. While the soul may be eternal, Living is not, let's play! Another example, of life's realities, is the following: Sometimes ago, while shopping at the Farmer's, Market for trees for my yard, I spotted some very attractive Blue Spruce trees. I told the person selling the trees that I would like to buy one. The person said to me: "you do know, don't you, that these blue spruces will not live in this climate?" My reply was: "In that case, why do you sell them here?" His reply was: "Because people buy them." Ok, I replied, I'll take two. The trees died the very next year; however, the honesty of one individual, still resides inside, yes, inside my soul.

Chapter One

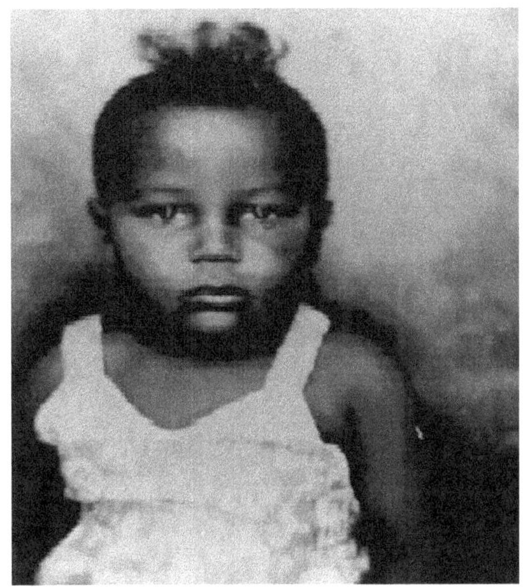

The Beginning

On a cool March night, in a small rural county in western Tennessee, a brave black woman, long past, the child-bearing years, squatted between a bed and a table and gave birth to a child. Having had several similar experiences, eleven to be exact, the woman tenderly, yet calmly, picked up the lump of humanity from the folded quilt that she had placed on the floor and held it. Pensively poised, the creamy-colored mother's thoughts wandered through her past, conveniently ignoring the many trials and tribulations that mothers sometimes face. Taking solace in her thoughts, the good times, the bad times, and the times that were so painful that her conscious mind would not even let her probe, she weakly smiled a smile, which reflected her hopes, dreams, fears, and nightmares.

Peering out through cracks in the broken-down, weather-worn share cropper's shack, this mother reflected upon the darkness which was so characteristic of the rural Tennessee countryside and whispered an almost incomprehensible prayer: "O"

Lord, thank you for this blessing, but please, no more."In an almost telepathic way, the newborn child seemed to sense the meaning of the mother's prayer and responded with a series of spasmodic jolts, causing the black woman to hastily add, "But if it's the Lord's will, bless my soul, and let it be."

"Lo," my father calling out to my oldest sister, "I reckon its time, go get Mr. Boomer. Your mammie be ready to go." Mr. Boomer lived down in the woods near our house and had delivered most of the black babies in the area. He was a thin, raw-boned white man who wore a black suit, no matter what the occasion. Upon reflection, the fact that he was also the self-appointed undertaker, may have accounted for the black suit that he wore. His favorite saying was "I heps 'em come n I heps 'em go out, 'n I get paid the same for both, nuthin." In any case, Lorraine, now in full pursuit of Mr. Boomer, shouted out to all that she passed " get outta the way, mamma gon has a baby and I ant got no time to talk, Mista

Bommer, Mista Bommer, come quick, da baby coming."

The sudden stirring of the slimy, blood-covered infant reminded the mother that she and the child were yet of one body, for the umbilical cord, which had furnished both physical and emotional nourishment to the glazed, mahogany, the infant was still attached to the child's swollen belly. Looking at the intestinal link, which had sustained both life and purpose for the child, the mother could not help but wonder whether or not this elongated mucous membrane had also communicated to the child the pain and sorrow she had felt while carrying him. She cringed as she painfully remembered the threats of the sun-blistered, tobacco-chewing landowner. Did he really intend to carry out his promise to kill the then unborn child in retaliation for the mothers in silence? She had no way of knowing that within six months she and the child would barely escape by hiding in a horse-drawn wagon filled with cotton under the darkness of the countryside.

The woman's warm hands trembled as she attempted to eradicate the ugly thoughts from her consciousness. Once again, the infant jolted, causing its long body to expand and contract almost as if it were growing in the woman's cradled arms. Dripping sweat from the mother's majestic face seemed to awaken the infant like spring rains liven budding trees. The baby's movements quickened as he attempted to expel mucus from his nostrils in order to inhale the warm, pungent, life-giving air into his tiny lungs. Sensing the child's pain, the woman instinctively yet skillfully covered the child's nose with her lips and sucked the slimy fluid from his nostrils. Although less than a minute had elapsed between the gentle thud of the child hitting the folded quilt and the mother literally breathing the breath of life into the child, it seemed more like an eternity.

The high squeal of the infant's first sound jolted the mother back into the cold reality of the moment. Still clutching the screaming infant to her breast, the woman slumped back into her bed exhausted. In a whisper that sounded more like a shout, " Ernest, Ernest, Y'all come in now."

I awoke to the familiar sound of barking dogs; cackling hens and the hollow sound of logs being chopped. Coupled with the mournful sound of an old Negro spiritual being chanted by someone unknown, yet familiar to me, quickened my senses. The ammoniated smell of chickens, horses, and cows was punctuated by the sweet smell of salt pork and homemade bread. From my straw-filled mattress, I peeked through a gap in the rough-cut planks of our shack into the sun-glazed, dusty yard. Standing there by the rail fence was my poppa chomping on his terrible smelling pipe. As the yellow-brown tobacco juice meandered down the corner of his mouth, I heard him mumble to my brother Gene that today was hog killing day. Much to the displeasure of my brother, my father went on to remind him that once again he would need to drink a cup of the fresh, warm blood from the slaughtered animal to help cure his asthma. Although I had witnessed this strange ritual before, it never failed to hold me spellbound. Looking back, I still do not understand the basis for my father's healing prescription, but when papa spoke, we all listened and followed.

Snuggling deeper into my bed, I attempted to freeze this scene momentarily to both preserve it and seal it in my memories forever. By the time I had finally released my sleeping place from the captivity of my small body, the other members of the family had gone about their daily sharecropper duties. My mother, braiding my sister's hair, looked the look of a skilled surgeon performing the most delicate operations, stared at me as I entered the room. Not speaking a word, she instructed me to take care of my biological needs and wash. As I left the room, my sister poked her tongue out at me as if she had somehow intercepted my mother's telepathic message and found joy in the fact that it was directed at me rather than her.

As I stepped out onto the rickety porch, I saw my father and brother walking slowly towards the barn. With the inquisitiveness, which only a three and a half-year-old could muster, I paused to observe an event, which was sure to be more interesting than my appointed trip to the outhouse. In almost script-like fashion, my father stopped suddenly and pointed toward the loft of the barn. Not having seen my father does anything suddenly, I felt that my expectation of something wonderful and exciting had already come to pass, there was more to come. From my vantage point on the porch, I could barely make out what my father was pointing to in the loft of the barn. As I moved off the porch and closer to my father, however, I saw what appeared to be a rope with red and yellow bands wrapped around one of the beams. As my brother rushed toward the house, my father put his large, map-like hand on my shoulder. With the assuredness, which the only papa can instill, I was certain that there was nothing to worry about; the snake would not harm me. My brother ran back from the house carrying what must have been the biggest shotgun ever. My body shook with pending anticipation of what was to follow. The thundering sound of the gun seemed to shake the entire countryside. I recall feeling the vibrations of the blast in father's muscular leg where my hand grasped his trousers. The snake, in an almost deliberate way, fell to the ground.

From the eyes of a child, I saw a big place, filled with images and faces of things and people that I knew, and felt safe with. From those same child's eyes, I saw and believed that everything I saw was about me and for me. My mother, father, and sisters and brothers were there just for me, and that was good, and the way that it should have been, from the eyes of a child.

The thundering sound of the shotgun caused the entire family to stop whatever they were doing and come running to the barnyard to see what was happening. The fearful expressions on the faces of my family members were both confusing and frightening to me. It was not until later that night, long after my father had shot the snake, which I was able to gain some understanding of the frightful looks evoked by the incident. I listened intently, almost without breathing. The story continued as a hush fell over the room. The fear in my sister's voice made my stomach tighten as she expressed how she felt the last time she had heard gunshots from a close distance. It seems that my father, who at least in my mind was mild-mannered and easy-going, was known to some whites as "one of those crazy, uppity niggas" because he stood up to anyone attempting to do harm to the family.

My image of my father, which was already bigger than life, became even larger, after listening to my sister retelling the story. My chest swelled as I moved closer to the circle of storytellers. For the benefit of my younger sisters and to my delight, my older sister retold the story that mamma had told them about how papa, upon his discharge from the army in 1922, organized a group of twenty-five or thirty "Negroes" for protection and retaliation. Whites had burned the shacks of several black families and had beaten as well as lynched several others. The hostile whites in the area, having heard of my father's efforts, had sent word throughout the county that no guns or ammunition be sold to "that Fuller nigga, or any of those other crazy niggas."

As a result of my father's actions, threats were made to both my father and my mother, who was outspoken and quick-tempered. On several occasions, my mother and father held off lynching parties by firing shots through the gaps in the planks of the house. They stayed alive by moving from place to place whenever the hostility got to the point where they could not protect the children or themselves. The last attack upon my father and mother came sometime after the birth of my youngest sister, Mae Ruth. It seems that a white man had called my mother a yellow bitch-nigga my mother, in words seldom spoken by ladies, retaliated with her own brand of verbal castration. She was backed up by my father and a twelve-gauge shotgun. Later that night the expected sounds of hoof beats and the shouts of several bloodthirsty riders sent my brothers and sisters, none of which were above the age of eighteen, scurrying under the straw-filled beds like frightened animals. My mother and father, in military fashion, took their positions on opposite sides of the house, with shotguns ready. As they had done on numerous occasions, they fired over the heads of their attackers. The next morning, however, a dead horse lay at the edge of the yard where the nightriders had gathered and fired their guns into the sides of my family's broken-down shack. My mother, pregnant with her fourth child, had obviously fired a little low on that occasion. At any rate, it was once again necessary for my family to move on. Later that night, as I drew the heavy quilt over my head, I sighed a sigh of both pride and exhaustion.

"From the eyes of a child, I looked forward to the next day's activities, which would surely end with the

family gathered around me, for family storytelling time, for and about me."

29

Chapter Two

Young Love

The next six months of my life were filled with events equally as sweet and rich in meaning for me as my barnyard episode. At the tender age of four, I discovered love, or more precisely, love discovered me. How does a four-year-old describe love? Does he think and speak of it in terms of the sudden surge of energy he feels when he sees the one, he loves? Or does he describe it in terms of the warmth he feels whenever he thinks of his love? No, from the eyes of a child, I rather think that he describes love in terms of how he feels when he sees the morning sun reflecting off the muddy stream which snakes its way through the bright rust and orange colored soil near his house. With baited anticipation, he awaits the sight and sound of the first blue jay or robin knifing through the morning air, in search of food. He listens for the rhetorical cooing of complacent doves, and he knows the feelings of love…further description is meaningless.

My love's name was Louise. Louise's skin was the color and texture of honey. Louise had eyes that danced like the ripples from raindrops falling on pools of standing water. Louise always smelled like jasmine, and lemonade, sweet and refreshing, but seldom tasted. Yes, I have my memories. And yes, at age four, and from the eyes of a child, I knew the feelings of love. I would later refine my description of love as a full-grown man upon meeting Jean, the only woman that I would ever really love.

While I was being captivated by the loveliness of my Louise, my world was changing. My brothers, one by one, left the home-house. Huston, at the age of thirteen, went away with the circus and enlisted in the army soon afterward. Gene Davis (Gen'nas) and James (Yang) followed work to another part of the state and my oldest sister moved-in with a family in another county, leaving me, my mother, father, and five sisters to carry on. There seemed to be a few happy memories after my family split up. Within three months I too would leave Tennessee for the big city of Detroit. It appeared my whole world had suddenly deserted me, leaving nothing but uncertainty and fear. There was to be no more building sand dooms down by the creek; there were to be no more fun-filled days with the family, and there was to be no more Louise. There were to be just my fears, my uncertainties, and me.

Chapter Three

City Living-A New Beginning

The shadows dancing on the wall of my Uncle Elmo's apartment located on what was "affectionately" known as the north end of Hastings Street caused my heart to quicken and my breathing to become erratic. I clinched the covers on my bed even tighter to reassure myself that my last line of defense was still intact. I watched in fear and amazement as the walls of the upstairs apartment became a panoramic stage hosting a wide-range of terrifying configurations, most of which I could not identify. This hideous production seemed to involve a cast of thousands. There were headless lions, snakes with two heads, and a vast assortment of other grotesque images that stirred my deepest fears. And of course, there were the clowns. The clowns who were supposed to bring laughter and joy to a four-year-old brought only more fear. I often wondered why the monsters all seemed to move in the same direction. Round and round, but in the opposite direction than the hands on my uncle's huge clock that stood as tall as my uncle. Round and round my maddening merry-go-round turned. I was sure that the monsters would spring off their carousel and onto my bed at the very next time around. Somehow, just when it seemed certain that I would be devoured by my shadowy roommates; they would disappear into the conclaves of the walls only to reappear in some other hideous form. I was a nightly patron of these fluorescent nightmares, however unwillingly. Sometimes to harness my fears, I would recast and choreograph my one-dimensional panoramic production into a more pleasant scenario.

My favorite production was the re-creation of my trip from Tennessee with my mother on the train. The flashing neon sign attached to the side of the apartment building near the window gave the illusion of two trains passing in the night, both flickering black and gray lights off and on as if to signal an end or beginning to something exciting which somehow never seemed to happen. If only shadows came in colors, maybe green, yellow, and sometimes red, then they would not have been so scary. But I had no such luck, they only appeared in benign shades of black, gray, and sometimes, off-white. Still, I managed to fall asleep despite it all.

The first two months in Detroit were good ones, although I did miss the other members of the family. My uncle Elmo did all he could to make the transition an easy one for my mother and me. He'd bring me candy and other nice things when he came home from work. His wife, my aunt, was, however, a different story. I somehow never felt welcome when she was around. Most of the time I'd simply pretend to play with my toys to avoid eye contact with her. But even then, I could feel her eyes probing my every move. My aunt was a very strong and dominant woman who always wore pants like a man. It didn't matter to me that she worked on the assembly line at the factory. I figured that she only did it to affirm the fact that she was in control of everything and everyone. *From the eyes of a child, I could only justify my aunt's indifference to me because she could not see herself as I did, through the eyes of a child.*

I had another uncle living nearby. Sometimes he'd take me to what seemed like a circus. There were animals, lots of people, and popcorn. In ever really knew my other uncle's real name. In fact, I still don't know his name. Everyone just called him Dad. Dad was much older than Uncle Elmo. He was much quieter, too. Dad couldn't talk, at least not so, that I could understand him. Funny thing though, everyone else in the family seemed to understand him just fine, especially Aunt Laura. I could never figure out whether Dad was a white man or just a light-skinned black man. Although it really didn't matter to me, we did get a lot of stares whenever we were together.

I especially liked going home with Dad. The apartment that Dad and my aunt shared, always smelled of good things to eat and my aunt always insisted that I eat until my little stomach bulged over the waistband of my trousers. Aunt Laura, or Dossier, as mother called her, was funny to look at and to talk to. She waddled like a duck when she walked and wore thick glasses that always sat on the bridge of her nose. My aunt never stopped talking from the time I got to her apartment until I left. I loved Aunt Laura for a lot of reasons, but mostly because she looked exactly like my mother. I remember Aunt Laura telling me on one of my visits, that she and my uncle Elmo had sent for my mother and me that they would soon send for the remainder of the family. She said that where we lived in the South was a very bad place because of some of those "bad" white people. While I didn't doubt the truth of what my aunt Laura said, I somehow didn't feel the same way about the place that I once called home. My aunt and uncle did eventually send for the remainder of the family. I thought that my life would once again be complete and happy, but it was not. The arrival of my five sisters and my father meant that my mother and I would have to move out of my Uncle Elmo's apartment and find a place large enough for the entire family, not an easy thing to do in a factory town during the war years. We spent nights sleeping in my uncle's big shiny car, with shoes, clothes and all.

Eventually, we found a place large enough for the entire family. We still had to sleep several to a bed. I recall how dark it was in our attic apartment. There were no windows or electric lights. The kerosene lamps, we had did not provides much light. Looking back, I now realize that the lack of illumination was a blessing in disguise, for any greater light would have served only to further depress the situation. There were no walls to speak of, only bare, smoked wooden structural frame of the attic. Our one bedroom was just big enough for my mother and father. The rest of us, my five sisters, and I slept on two mattresses laid on the floor. I remember that my mother would always caution us about making too much noise. She said that the people downstairs complained about the noise we kept up. Most of the time after the sun went down, we would huddle around the dim kerosene lamp like frightened animals patiently awaiting sleep and eventually, daylight. Days were brief, but the nights seemed to go on forever. In order to use the toilet, we had to go downstairs to the other family's flat. Our food was also cooked downstairs and brought upstairs in pots for us to eat. Although our family thought that we had made a move upwards in our standard of living, I had my own reasons for doubting their conclusions. Still, I, like the other members of my family, made the necessary adjustments and life went on. It really wasn't so bad, once I got used to it. *Anyway, five-year-old children adjusted and forgot quite rapidly, didn't they?*

My father soon found a job in the foundry and my mother went to work at the automobile plant. Things were really looking up for us. I remember thinking how rich we were when I received my weekly allowance, a quarter from each of my parents. Soon, we moved into another flat with electric lights and even our own bathroom. Within a year I had completely adjusted to my new life in the city and all but forgotten about Tennessee. The neighborhood, where we lived was a poor one located on the lower east side of the city. Except for the white insurance men and the Jewish merchants, it was an all-black community except for the Polish family that lived across the alley. They too were poor, but the son, Billie, was my best friend and neither of us knew or cared that we were poor. Still, no one seemed to notice whenever someone different came around.

Chapter Four

Hastings Street
(Black Bottom)

Our house was one block from Hastings Street. Hastings was alive and exciting. I recall hearing grown-ups saying that a person could get or do anything down on Hastings Street. Although the street itself stretched from the river to the outer edges of the lower east side, the section near where we lived was generally considered to be the heart of the street. There were small grocery stores, movie houses, pawnshops, clothing stores, and last, but not least, the beer gardens and churches. *This was my new world, and at six, I felt more than able to cope with it.*

I specifically recall the Saturday nights on Hastings Street. On the corner of Hastings and Garfield was "Cozy Corner," a very well-known tavern or beer garden, as they were called in those days. All the pretty ladies of the night would frequent Cozy's, with their fancy clothes, liquid hips, and ruby-red lips. At the age of six, and from the eyes of a child, I naturally had no understanding of or appreciation for what role these labors of love played in the scheme of things, but I sensed that they were forbidden fruits for six-year-olds and some grown-ups as well. Some of my friends and I had fun peeping around corners at them as they walked with their men, friends up the stairs to whatever. We'd laugh and giggle as if we knew the significance of what was about to happen.

There were also the men in Cozies. They all wore big hats and long shinny Stacy Adams shoes with big metal plates on the heels and the toes that made the sound of someone dancing when they walked. My brother James, who was known as "Big Jim," was very much a part of Cozy's regulars. Big Jim was a lady's man. He had long black wavy hair, a big mustache, and very small eyes. I was proud of my brother because most of the ladies in the neighborhood thought that he was something special and flirted with him constantly. My brother liked Mattie with her big brown eyes and long coal-black hair. I liked Mattie to, but for different reasons. On the corner of the alley was an ice cream parlor and that was where Mattie worked. All I had to do was to go to the counter, sit and stare into Mattie's big brown eyes. Before long, Mattie would bring me the biggest double-dipped ice cream cone imaginable. Yes, I really liked Mattie for all the right reasons. Big Jim and Mattie would later marry and have thirteen children. On the corner and a couple of doors down from the ice cream parlor where pretty Mattie worked was "Bloody Mary's" beer garden. The name befitted the place quite nicely. On any Saturday night, one could see at least two or three fights at Bloody Mary's. As strange as it now seems, nobody was ever seriously hurt. They would just cut-up each other and come back the next Saturday the best of buddies with the week before all but forgotten. It was a well-known fact by the people in the community that Bloody Mary's did not have as much class as did Cozy's and sometimes, that was the reason for some of Saturday's fights.

Saturday night fights at Cozy's and Bloody Mary's was accented by loud blues music, which seemed to permeate all the beer gardens along Hastings Street. The likes of B.B. King, Muddy Waters, and Howling Wolf constituted a very important part of my musical repertoire during my early years. Blues, affectionately known as "Gut-Bucket" music, had some competition from the gospel music being played in the churches sprinkled among the beer gardens and Chitin Shacks. Groups, like the Mighty Clouds of Joy, the Soul Stirrers, and the Five Blind Boys, more than held their own down on Hastings Street. Somehow, there seemed to be a peaceful co-existence between all the divergent elements on our street. Yes, there was a place for all down on Hastings Street. The preachers, the pimps, the hustlers, and the ladies of the night were among the most generous when the collection plates were passed on Sunday morning, cleansing them of their sins and transgressions from the night before. And, to the satisfaction of the true Christians, the sinners, pimps, ladies of the night, and the gamblers, were the most graphic testifiers. The prodigal sons and the wayward children would all weep and shout with the best on Sunday morning, down on Hastings Street, in the houses of God.

Yes, Hastings Street was quite a place, not perfect, but no less special to me and a very real part of my world. Little else existed for me outside of the people and places around Hastings Street. Many dreams and dreamers lived and died on that street. There were a certain fulfillment and sense of belonging associated with living there. Everyone seemed to know everybody else and everyone knew where they fitted in on the social scale. Yes, there was a social scale on Hastings Street, not based on income, size of your house, or what kind of car you drove. In fact, few families owned or lived in houses or had cars. No, social standing was based on several factors. Age was one of the highest-ranking indicators of placement on the hierarchy.

Saturdays were also special for me and the other children on or near Hastings Street, mainly because Saturday was movie day at the Willis movie theater, which was nestled between the beer joints and houses of God. For a quarter, you could see two cowboy movies, a Flash Gordon episode, two cartoons, the latest news chips, soda and a bag of chips.

Chapter Five

The Projects

Several blocks down the street, nestled on the edge of Cozy's and Bloody Mary's, set the Brewster Projects. Like most public housing projects in those days, you had to know somebody in order to feel safe walking there. Even better, was being related to someone, like a cousin or an uncle. Otherwise, you always felt like something bad was about to happen to you. More times than not, you would be right. Although the entire area surrounded by Hastings Street was populated by poor people, the Brewster Projects represented the slums of the ghetto. Still, like all of Hastings Street, the projects possessed its own charm and style. There were those, however, who would take serious issue with my perspective. Nevertheless, to speak publicly against project people, was equivalent to walking on the edge of a razor blade, only bloodier. Located in the center of the projects was Brewster Center, the spawning ground for athletes and entertainers from across the city. The "has-beens," the "wannabe's, and the "never would be's" all gathered at the Brewster Center for their days in the sun.

I vividly recall the sounds and smells of the Brewster Center Gym, which was nearly always filled with people from different parts of the city. The syncopated sounds of worn leather, the repetitive tapping of the light punching bag, the rhythmic thug and pounding of the heavy bag, and the symphonic sounds of a chorus of rope skippers were augmented by a series of grunts and moans of the young hopefuls as they exchanged punches, boxed with images of themselves, or engaged in a wide assortment of body-building and mind-dulling exercises. The musty air reeked with odors of physical exhaustion, unwashed bodies, and the stale smell of Lucky Strikes, Camels, and Phillip Morris cigarette smoke. All of this served as a very effective backdrop for the constant junk talking which was a prerequisite for acceptance into the inner circles of the Brewster Center elite. I listened intently to the older boys sitting near me and dreamed of the day when I would take my place among them. The excitement of the verbal sparring prompted one of the smaller boys to confidently proclaim to be the "Best nigga" within the room. A chorus of retorts followed his proclamation, "nigga, you must be either blind or crazy." This scenario continued for what seemed like hours with each member of the inner circle taking their turn at verbal castration, but it was all in fun. These kinds of friendly confrontations were taking place all over the center. Nobody ever really took them seriously or got mad. It was just a part of being a member of the Brewster Center family.

Sitting there in the gym, my thoughts drifted in and out of the gym, the inner circle, and into the lives of the people living in the housing projects. It was both sad and confusing as to why all the units were painted in the same benign shades of desperation and despair, gray and darker gray. The cinder block walls gave the appearance of a prison, one brick stacked on top of another, going nowhere, letting nothing in, and letting nothing out. My despair, however, did not seem to be shared by the people who lived in the Brewster Projects. There was a certain pride exhibited by them toward their dwellings. There was no apparent shame connected to the fact that the first criteria for living in the projects were that you had to be classified as poor and generally receiving government assistance. Still, generations after generations were born there and died there, and life went on in the Brewster Projects and in the Brewster Center near Hastings Street.

The garbage and the trash-strewn near the entranceways never seemed to get collected. The broken windows and doors never seemed to get repaired. The elevator walls were always filled with various suggestions about where to go, what to do when you got there, and who to take with you. Although my reading vocabulary was limited at age six, I could only sense that the spelling and grammar were correct. I was only six and just about to finish the first grade, so, what did I know? The elevators, with all their graffiti, always worked. They worked although they generally smelled as if someone had recently vomited, urinated, or performed some other act in them equally objectionable.

There were lots of children my age living in the projects. Most ran around and through the brick buildings without shoes. Shoes were saved for school, church or funerals. Funny though, nobody ever cut their feet on the pieces of broken glass that seemed to be just everywhere. We were the children of Hastings Street, strong, independent, and street-wise. It was often said that although the children on Hastings Street looked a lot like each other and the milkman, mailman, and the Iceman, more than a few looked like whoever was buying the food for that week.

Inside the Projects were even more exciting. The reverberating sounds of unattended babies crying, women screaming at husbands who couldn't account for the shortage in their paychecks, and husbands cursing for the same reasons was accented by what seemed like a thousand photographs, all playing different records at the same time. Over in the corner of the hallway six or seven teenage boys singing, each in a different key and meter sounded good to me. I often visualized myself singing with such makeshift superstars of the ghetto. In another corner of the same hall, a group of boys and men were standing and kneeling in a circle shooting craps. "Four for Joe," "five and no Jive," "ten for Big Ben," were the typical sinner's prayers emanating from the gambler's circle. Propped in another corner near the stairway was a tall teenage boy talking to a more than interested teenage girl. Down the hallway and around the corner several highly intoxicated construction workers and factory workers each, in turn, passed a bottle of cheap wine and boasted about the intricacy of their jobs. Periodically, an upstanding senior citizen would curse the group of drunks in the "name of the Lord," present one of several mini-sermonettes, threaten to either call the police or tell the wives of the men involved, and quickly slam their doors where they would continue to give their undivided attention to trying to figure out the next day's number.

In the basement of the building was the laundry room. Several women were discussing in very serious tones, the plight of their families and neighbors. In another part of the room, several other women were having their hair straightened or curled in readiness for Fridays and Saturday's house parties or appointed trips to either Cozy's or Bloody Mary's, or one of several other lessons known beer gardens or taverns down on Hastings Street. The smell of smoke from the burning of hair being straighten, coupled with the smoke from cigarettes appeared to go unnoticed by the group of women and men holding bible class in a small space adjacent to the laundry room. A short distance from the laundry room a group of teenagers was preparing for a party, which was always held in the basement. Generally, the extent of this preparation was limited to an adjustment of the volume of the record player to the maximum, removing all but two or three chairs, and hiding all but one small blue light bulb. These scenes were essentially occurring in each of the larger public housing project buildings near, in, and around Brewster Center.

Saturday mornings in the Projects were always unfriendly reminders of the night before. Unattended babies still cried because parents were sleeping late. Phonographs still played and a few of the losers from the crap game were still arguing over the five dollars remaining between all of them. Slumped on the floor near the upstanding senior citizen's door, lay one of the factory workers with an empty wine bottle clutched gently to his chest. Inside the senior citizen's unit, the taunt smell of lucky incense made it difficult for the old lady to give her policy slips their proper attention. Downstairs in the laundry area, empty jars of Dixie Peach hair grease were the only reminders of the creativeness that had taken place on the heads of many women during the previous evening. Further down the hall in the party room, lay cigarette butts, wine bottles, and crushed paper cups, all spoils of a really good time.

Saturday morning was also a bill-collection time in the projects. The expressions on the faces of the white insurance men, and their smiles covered up by indifference and even disdain gave me a most unpleasant feeling. Although I didn't quite understand the meaning of my feelings, I was sure that they had something to do with the fact that we were all colored and bill collectors were always all white. Bill collectors never knocked on our doors; they simply walked in with wide plastic smiles and looks of uneasiness. They seldom sat without first brushing the place where they were to sit. Our mothers and fathers were referred to by their first names and the children got pats on our heads like pets. *In my lighter moments, I figured that they were, in their own way, attempting to be friendly. Still, the feelings of hurt were ever present.*

The penetrating sound of the ring buzzer, signaling the end of the fifth bout, ended my daydreaming in the Brewster Projects and reminded me that I would have to hurry if I was to beat the darkness home. Racing down the stairs, I spotted Flash. Flash was the best tap dancer on the east side, maybe the entire city. Flash was tall, skinny, and very black. But boy, Flash could dance! You never saw him without his tap-dancing shoes hung over his shoulders. Flash would start dancing as soon as anyone stopped to look. Although he made a few dollars dancing up and down Hastings Street, everybody knew that Flash was dancing for Flash, not for the money. Flash quickly did one of his patterned turns and kicks and ended with what appeared to be a painful split and winked at me. Boy, Flash could dance! Unfortunately, I had no time to stop and watch because; I was losing my race with the darkness. Dashing out of the gym door, I ran smack into one of the older bullies of the neighborhood. Grabbing me by the arm, he quickly explained the facts of life to me, which I loosely understood to mean, "Do it again and I'm going to beat your ass raw." Little did he know that compared to the whipping that my mother would give me if I got home after dark, his ass whipping was nothing. Still, the better part of fear and good sense convinced me, that I should avoid any further confrontation with the bully. As I made what was known on the streets as a "country break," I took one backward glance to see if the bully was coming after me, he wasn't. Turning the first corner, I hoped that he would not remember my face and later send his younger brother, who was also a bully to get me. As I turned the next corner onto Hastings Street, I spotted my brother, Big Jim. Breathing a sigh of relief, I slowed to a medium sprint and attempted to compose myself to not cause my brother concern. "Chest," my brother called. "Mama's looking for you with a green switch." Racing past my brother, I searched my mind for a good excuse. Just then, I spotted my sister coming out of the corner store carrying a small bag. There is a God, I thought. Without breaking stride, I grabbed the bag from Mae

Ruth's arm and immediately began a conversation of little substance but great purpose. Mae Ruth and the store would be my excuse and not a bad one, I thought. Too many times, I had felt the sting of the green switch. The folds of newspaper strategically placed inside my pants helped to block some of the pain but little of the intent. Somehow, my mother never seemed to notice the odd sound made by the switch striking the newspapers inside my pants. I figured that mothers couldn't hear as well as six-year-olds. Walking up the stairs with my sister, I reflected on the day's activities in anticipation of tomorrow.

I could have spent the rest of my life down on Hastings Street, where summers seemed endless, autumns lasted as long as the bright orange and yellow leaves, and winters consisted of freshly fallen snow, Christmas, and toys. Unfortunately, the summers did end, the bright leaves of autumn did turn brown and wrinkle were blown away or crushed, down on Hastings Street. The folds of crisp blue-white snow did melt and turn to slush, Christmas passed, toys broke, and I turned seven down on Hastings Street, where the unspoken rules made sense, unforeseen events were predictable, yet surprising, and even strangers were known and welcomed down on Hastings Street.

Chapter Six

Garfield Street

At the age of eight, my family moved from one part of Hastings Street to a street that crossed Hastings, Garfield Street. What seemed like a move that was miles away from our house on Hastings, was no more than six or seven blocks. I can still visualize the cobble-stone streets, the horse watering troughs, and the sound of the iceman's wagon, as it moved down the cobble-stone streets. We moved into a basement of a two-family flat, which was a converted coalbin. The fact that the floor was dirt was concealed by the lack of light because there were no windows in the former coal bin. The only light came from a single light bulb hanging from a wire in the main part of the basement. In retrospect, the absence of light was a blessing for it, not only to hide the dirty floor but the coal dust that had accumulated over the years. Of course, there were no toilet facilities or running water to drink or to wash hands or other body parts; still, it was home to me, my mother and father, my three sisters, and my oldest sister's three children.

Garfield was not a bad place to live. An eight-year-old can find fun in almost any place. After all, what could go wrong, when you're only eight years old? Well, with this eight-year-old, something did go wrong. I was given or maybe acquired some wrong information about White people. It was a common urban legend that White people were afraid of Blacks and would not fight them. My best and only friend, whose name was Billy, was White and he was neither afraid of Black people nor afraid to fight them. On this one occasion, I wanted to confirm the urban legend about White people. Who better to test the legend then Billy, my best friend? I suggested to Billy that we should have a boxing match. Bad idea Billie, being the friend that he was, allowed me to throw the first punch. With all of the power that I could gather, I hit Billy right on his jaw. I just knew that this punch would end the match, not so. Three things happened: Billy's jaw turned bright red, Billy shook his head, as if to dismiss the punch, and said to me "Come-on guy, give me your best." At that point, I resorted to another urban legend, "When all else fails, say that you hear your mother calling you" and head for home. "So much for urban legends," I'm thinking to myself, as I crossed the alley heading home. Even from the eyes of a child, *I could understand that you should not believe everything that you hear, especially when what you hear is referred to as a "legend."*

At the age of nine, my life-experiences revolved and evolved on or near Garfield Street. On Garfield Street, everyone knew everyone else, their hopes, problems, failures, and their successes. Family secrets were well known and discussed throughout the neighborhood. For example, everyone knew why Johnson's teenage girl suddenly went down south to visit relatives for several months before reappearing with her cousin's infant child that the family had decided to take care of as if they needed one more child to add to the seven already staying in the two-bedroom flat. Ironically, some families still living in the south would send their pregnant unmarried teenage daughters to northern cities to live with relatives to give birth to their child. Life's lesson here is that many of the accepted stereotypes regarding the value systems of poor blacks living in the north or south were incorrect. In effect, having children out of wedlock was taboo in black families and was therefore looked upon with shame. Even though there was family shame associated with young black girls having babies without being married, there was no less love for the child. The love of children within black culture, while a historical fact, is, unfortunately not accepted or believed in the larger white communities.

Christmas on Garfield Street was special, not because we all had Christmas trees loaded with pretty, colorful lights and lots of presents for everyone. In fact, I don't recall ever seeing a Christmas tree at anyone's house during the holiday season. People on Garfield could not afford to buy Christmas trees, or gifts, not to mention Christmas lights. Still, despite the poverty, there was a certain joy in our neighborhood during Christmas. Much of the joy had to do with the good fellows. The Good fellows is a charitable organization that has existed since 1912 for the expressed purpose of serving underprivileged children. On Christmas morning, the Good fellows would give each family a Christmas box for each of the children in the respective households. The Good fellows' Christmas box contained a shirt or blouse, long-john underwear, a box of hard candy, and a coupon for a pair of shoes.

We were all poor and Black, except for my best friend Billy, who was poor, but White, and the three polish sisters who owned the corner store that we all, with affection, referred to as "The Three Sisters." They were also White, like Billy, but they were not poor. The sisters lived upstairs over their store and seldom ventured out beyond the store and their upstairs apartment. They were each short, not exceeding five feet in height, and always wore a scarf on their heads. They moved in unison as if they were of one body. I don't recall ever seeing fresh vegetables in the Three Sisters store, only vegetables in cans. Still, most people in the neighborhood shopped at the store and had a running credit account with the three sisters. All accounts were kept by the sisters on a small three-inch tablet where the sisters would use a very short pencil to keep track of each family's credit purchases. On the first day of each month, the Three Sister's store would be quite busy cashing welfare and social security checks and collecting what was owed for groceries bought during the previous month. In retrospect, the sisters could not have been poor, since they had enough money to cash welfare and social security checks. In any case, there were always arguments between the sisters and various families regarding either the amount owed or the fact that a family could not pay the entire amount owed for the previous month. These were the only times that the sisters were heard speaking to each other in their native polish tongue.

"ci ludzie są szaleni I leniwi," translation: {These people are crazy and lazy}.

Somehow, differences between three sisters and various families worked themselves out, and life continued for me down on Garfield Street, where the only excitement occurred on Friday and Saturday nights at the house parties or fish-fries, as the people on the block called them. Although the stated purpose for the Friday and Saturday fish fries was to sell fish sandwiches and fish dinners, the real reason was to drink, dance, and meet new friends, in short, to party. It still is a mystery, how so many people were able to get into the limited space. Yes, the music played was way too loud, fresh air or ventilation of any kind was limited to an open window, and the pungent smell of alcohol and Lucky Strike cigarette smoke made breathing and seeing difficult. Yet, nobody complained or seemed to mine. The problems didn't surface until the next morning when some of the men couldn't account for the money that they no longer had or the lipstick on their shirts. From the perspective of an eight-year-old, going on nine, I could hardly wait until I was old enough to experience what seemed to be so much fun.

Chapter Seven

Momma and Poppa

On one of those mornings following the Friday and Saturday night parties, the neighborhood bully, who was referred to as Hawk, made a big mistake. He called my mother a "yellow bitch." It's worth noting at this point, that Hawk looked like the proverbial bully. He was over six feet tall, narrow-chested, and never seemed to have shaved. My father, who was by all accounts, considered to be an easy-going mild-mannered man, was sitting on an empty milk carton smoking his pipe. When Hawk called my mother a yellow bitch, it was like the entire block stopped what they were doing and waited for, what everyone knew was going to be interesting. Again, it's worth noting at this point, that this was before my mother "found Jesus," so, she was neither submissive nor ladylike. My mother gave Hawk a verbal tongue lashing that would make a Christian repent, causing Hawk to tell my mother that he was going to beat her yellow ass. My father calmly put his pipe in his shirt pocket and took an empty milk jar from the crate that he was sitting on.

Exhibiting little emotion, poppa hit Hawk across his forearm. Blood went everywhere, but mostly on Hawk. The thin broken glass from the milk bottle opened Hawk's arm from his hand to his elbow. The site of Hawk, bleeding like a half-slaughtered hog, running for home, made my day. My mother posed a question for Hawk as he ran for home: "How your gonna beat my yellow ass with one black arm?" So much for the neighborhood bully. From that point forward, Hawk lost the title of "bully" and would crossover to the other side of the street before passing our house. Once again, my chest swelled with pride for my father.

My father was only twelve years old when he first saw my mother, Effie when she was a six-month-old baby. My grandmother was changing my mother's diaper, when Ernest, my father, walked in and pronounced "that little red baby is going to be my wife one day." My father went to the army, and when he returned, he took his bird, and his dog to find my mother, the love of his life. When he arrived at my mother's house, he told her to put on her dress, because it was time to get married. The two of them jumped in the car, my father in the driver's seat, with his bird on his shoulder, and his bride-to-be, who took her place in the back seat, because the dog was riding "shotgun," and refused to move. My mother and father were married that day at the general store, on August 5th, 1919.

My father was a soft-spoken man of few words. Since my father seldom said much, it was easy for me to remember the three things, he said to me. The first was a piece of advice, as a very young child, living in Detroit. "Boy doesn't touch that hot stove," I did, and still have the scars to prove that the stove was hot. The second thing he said to me was more of an order, then a piece of advice: "Boy, don't bring home a dark-skinned woman," and I didn't. The third thing that my father told me was more of an assessment of me, rather than advice: "boy, you don't have a "partiality" about yourself." It was not until several years later, in fact, I was completing my master's degree in clinical psychology, that it came to me, what my father was telling me when he told me that I didn't have any "partiality." He was trying to tell me that I had no "personality." Again, my father was right, and I have scars to prove it. Later in life, I told my sisters about my father's order not to bring home a dark-skinned woman. They told me that our poppa had told them the same thing, except he told them "not to bring home no piece of coal," meaning, no dark-skinned man, however, they all did. It's difficult to blame my father for his attitude regarding skin tone. After all, the negative beliefs about black skin had been bred into him from birth. The fact that the twelve children that he had fathered generally reflected a broad range of skin tones, ranging from very dark to "high yellow," did not appear to cause him any dissonance. He treated us all the same, without regard to the tone of our skin. That is not to say, however, there were not skin-tone issues between some of the siblings. One of my sisters would often refer to one or more of the darker-skinned brothers or sisters as "black dogs," although she was the darkest of us all. *Again, "self-hate" has been, and remains an issue among black people. It is in fact, likely one of the main factors impacting our journey from childhood to adulthood.*

Unlike my father, my mother was out-spoken but generous. I recall that she would often call less fortunate people to share whatever we had to eat, which in many instances, was very little. She was a big proponent of education and was totally committed to doing whatever necessary to ensure that; I had everything I needed to attend and finished high school.

Even though we were poor, and spent various periods receiving public assistance, she managed to provide private music lessons for me. In addition, she had somehow managed to buy me a car while I was in high school by doing day-work for wealthy people in the Gross Point community outside of the Detroit area. My mother taught herself to play piano, as the saying goes, "playing by ear." My mother loved to play the piano with anyone who wanted to sing. She never worried about what the song was, or what musical key the song was in. She knew how to play one tune, and would play that one tune, no matter what song a person wanted to sing. My mother was not only religious; she was also spiritual. In short, she believed in doing right by everyone regardless of who they were or what they looked like. She believed that being clean was next to Godliness, and she spent much of her typical day proving her beliefs. The site of anything dirty would cause her to break out in a rash. Back then, the rash was referred to as "Nella-rash," Nella-rash is a form of eczema that may have several causes, such as dust mites, bacterial, fungal, viral, or parasitic infections. Some research indicates that skin rashes maybe partly psychosomatic. In any case, my mother associated the rash with filth and filth with sin. Of all the people that I associated with or new on a personal level, it was my mother that not only helped to form and shape my soul, but she was also, and will always

remain the essence of my soul.

Chapter Eight

High school and Girls

By the time I started high school, my parents moved the family to a much nicer neighborhood than the one we lived in on Garfield Street. It was a two-family flat located on the east side of Detroit, near the river, and a long way from Hastings, the Brewster Center projects, and Garfield Street. Although only Black people lived in the neighborhood, the high school that I attended, Eastern High School, consisted of mostly White kids. All the teachers and counselors were white up until my senior year when a young Black female teacher, Miss McNeil came. And I must confess, I did not view Miss McNeil through the eyes of a child, she was "wet-dream" material! Miss McNeil must have been in her mid-twenties, pecan-brown, with a body that would make most women hate her. But, at age seventeen, what would I know? At that age, I had no real context or experience from which I could draw from regarding women, with one, maybe two or three exceptions, Mary Johnson, who I knew in middle school and Ellen who was my high school sweetheart, at least I thought Ellen was my high school sweetheart, and Dorothy. Like Ms. McNeill, Mary Johnson had a body, even at age fourteen, that showed promise for future "mischievous" acts. She was flirtatious to the point that made you feel that you had had sex with her, which, darn it, I never did, but more about Mary later. Ellen, unlike Ms. McNeil, and Mary Johnson, did not have a great body, nor was she flirtatious, but, as I later found out, she was more devilish than the other two combined. In fact, it was Ellen that broke my seventeen-year-old heart and taught me one more "life lesson." Let me explain. Ellen and I did not attend the same high school. She attended Cass Tech high school that was for high achieving students who were bound for college. The most Ellen and I ever did; was some heavy petting in my car. I never tried to go any further with Ellen because I just knew that she was an angel without wings. I later found out, however, why she had no wings!

Ellen told me that she was going to a house party on the Westside on Saturday and that I should meet her there. Sound good, so I agreed to meet her at the house-party. When I arrived at the house where the party was being held, I noticed that there were only a few cars parked in the driveway or on the street. I entered the house and was told that the party was being held downstairs in the basement, which was typical back in the day, however, I did not hear any music or "party noise" typically associated with house parties. Again, no problem. When I entered the room, I noticed that there were no girls, except for Ellen, my high school sweetheart. She and five boys were playing cards at a table. No problem, the party was probably late getting started. As I moved closer to the table, I noticed that the card game was "strip poker," and my high school sweetheart, Ellen, was losing badly. We have a problem! I was both shocked and heart-broken. I had never seen the parts of Ellen's body that was on display as a result of her loss in strip poker. It was at that point that I realized *why she had no wings! The "Life-Lesson" learned here was never date an angel with no wings. "Wing" is a metaphor for reputation or deeds. Unfortunately, in many cases, we have no idea about a person's reputation or deeds. As a result, we generally only have isolated observations or "feelings" to guide us, and, when you think about it, "feelings" are pretty good indicators of character or "Wings."*

After the heart-break incident with Ellen, I had yet, another high school girlfriend setback. My best friend, in high school, was Lewis Whitman and Naomi, Lewis's girlfriend. The three of us did everything together. Lewis was a year or two older than me, and three years older than Naomi, who absolutely adored Lewis. Lewis was one of the most popular boys in school, He was well over six-feet tall, and considered a great catch by most of the girls at Eastern High School. I liked Mary Johnson, who attended another high school on the west side of Detroit. Ballroom dancing was the rage in Detroit at that time. So, Lewis, Naomi and I would go to the Madison Ballroom on Friday nights, on this night, Neyome did not go to the dance with us. I told Lewis that my girlfriend, Mary Johnson, was going to meet us there. On the way to the dance, Lewis bet me that he could "pull" Mary. In short, he could take Mary away from me, although he had never met Mary. "No chance!" I quickly responded. So, at the dance, Lewis asked me to show Mary to him, and I did a bad move. Lewis danced with Mary through one record, after which he brought Mary back to me, and ask her to tell me something. Mary told me that she was sorry, but she liked Lewis now and we were finished. Needless to say, my young ego and self-worth, was shattered.

After my best friend took my girl, just because he could, while Lewis and I remained friends, I never actually trusted Lewis again. Years later, after we all graduated from high school, our paths would cross again. I had joined the Marines for three years, came back to Detroit for a short period, married, and moved to Chicago. Lewis and Neyome were married, and had two daughters, and had also moved to Chicago, not too far from where Jean and I lived. Although I would occasionally stop by to see Lewis, the girls, and Neyome, our friendship was never the same.

The incident with Ellen and Mary caused me to reassess my approach to high school dating. I attended lots of dances in hopes of meeting other girls, with little success. I was considered by most of the high school girls as a "square." I would go to the dances alone and leave alone. I noticed that the guys who wore the flashy clothes, talked a lot of "stuff," always had plenty of girls around them and seldom left the dances with less than one or sometimes two girls with them. I, on the other hand, always dressed like an Ivey league schoolboy and talked very little to anyone. In fact, if you need more verification, I was voted in the high school yearbook as the "Ideal High School Boy." I maintained that image throughout high school, college, and well into adulthood. I did notice, however, that the older I got, the more I noticed that women who were about something, were more drawn to "ideal, serious type man than to the flashy, fast-talkers type.

After I severed my relations with Ellen, I met Dorothy, my second-high school sweetheart. Like Ellen, Dorothy was somewhat petite with a look of innocence that few nuns could match. Dorothy was from Georgia and was a preacher's daughter with a "Scarlet O'Hara" southern accent. Dorothy, like many southern women, used eye contact and an exaggerated southern drawl to make promises that they had no intentions to keep, although, I must confess, Dorothy tried.

Dorothy's path and mine would cross again years after we both graduated from high school. I had spent three years in the Marine Corps, returned to Detroit for a short period, and moved to Chicago. One weekend night, I was in a small bar on the Southside of Chicago in the Chatham area. On this night, the club was more crowded with women than usual. They seem to be having some sort of celebration party. Sitting at the head of the table was a petite woman who spoke with a distinct southern drawl. Yes, it was Dorothy. We recognized each other at about the same time. After several polite hugs, Dorothy explained to me that she had returned to Atlanta after graduation and had gotten her degree from Spelman College in Atlanta. Dorothy revealed to me that she was celebrating her upcoming marriage scheduled for the next day and that she would love for me to attend the wedding. I did go to Dorothy's wedding that next day. She looked beautiful, and I was proud of her for being Dorothy, southern drawl and all.

Chapter Nine

Jean

On July 24th, 1960, at the age of 21, I completed my three-year service in the Marine Corps and headed back home to Detroit. Although it was great being back home with my mother, father, and a host of sisters and brothers, I still felt like a marine, meaning that I did nothing without purpose and structure. After spending my first couple of weeks back in Detroit, I begin to feel that there was something missing in my life, like purpose and progression towards achieving a goal or goals. My mother, who was always a strong proponent of education and had only completed the ninth grade, suggested that I must investigate further my education. Following her advice, I enrolled in a business college because I thought that I wanted to be an accountant. Why, I had no idea, especially since I never had much money to count or manage, and I had only taken general math in high school. Nevertheless, it made my mother extremely proud and happy that she finally had one of her twelve children to attend college. Seeing my mother happy gave me purpose and attending college gave me structure. Mission accomplished!

My first couple of weeks of attending college classes was somewhat less than exciting. Learning how to apply credits and debts could not be compared to the classes I had taken in the Marine Corps where I was taught to inject myself with watered down chemical to counteract the effects of nerve gas, or how to kill by driving the bones in a person's nose up into his brain. One day, after class, I took the elevator down to the main floor to the restaurant to have lunch. When I stepped out of the elevator, I saw this round-faced girl with bangs just standing there, apparently, waiting to take the elevator up to the floor above. She seemed focused and unintentionally sophisticated. In short, I thought she was stunning. Not knowing what to do or say next in order to further delight in her presence, in the most innocent voice possible, I asked her if she knew where the restaurant was. She nodded, but did not smile, and told me that I would have to leave the building and go around the corner to the small cafe because the college restaurant was closed for some reason. Feeling somewhat dejected, but not rejected, I thanked her and headed toward the exit. Before I reached the exit, I heard a voice say, "wait a minute, I'll show you." Remembering one of my mother's favorite prayers, in silence, I shouted: "Thank you Jesus, and bless my soul." "The next day, around the same time of the previous day, I took the same elevator down to the first floor to the college restaurant for lunch." The elevator ride down one floor seemed like forever. Would she be there? Would she even remember me? I somehow felt her presence even before the elevator stopped, and the door opened. She was there. "Be cool" I'm thinking to myself, "and breathe," I did neither. Her name was Jean. Cassie Jean Prince, to be exact.

For the next several months, we had lunch together in that small café near the college. It was during our lunch meetings and other dates that she told me that she had graduated from high school at age 15 and was now 17 and would be finishing her secretarial program within a couple of months. She also informed me that I might want to attend the end of the school year dance that Friday for graduating students. That, of course, sounded great to me since I wanted to be with her whenever I could.

The dance was held in a small auditorium at the college. I arrived at the college after nine that evening. When I entered the room, I heard a piano playing and a female voice. Jean was standing by the piano singing my funny valentine. I froze in the very spot where I had entered the room. It was as though I was the only one in the room, and she was singing just to me. I knew at that moment that this was the woman that I loved, and nothing could ever change that. It was also at that point that I had to face up to the reality of my situation. Namely, I was not working, living with my parents, and basically making it from the small unemployment check that I was receiving. There were simply no jobs to be had in Detroit at that time. As a result, I decided to move to Chicago where my sister and brother lived in hope of finding a job. I'll never forget the night that I told Jean of my plans to move to Chicago. I don't know what I expected her reaction to being, but it was not what I ever thought possible. She told me that she also had family in Chicago and that she wanted to go with me. Jean's mother didn't object to Jean's moving to Chicago with me. According to Jean's mother, even as a child, Jean was always mature and independent. In fact, according to her mother, Jean a kind of raised herself. When she was nine years old, she found a wagon to earn money taking people's groceries to home. She did not use her money to buy candy as most nine-years-old did. Instead, she saved most of the money she earned and used some to buy small food items for the family.

When Jean and I arrived in Chicago, we moved in with my sister Cora and her husband Joe. Although we pretended to sleep in separate rooms, everyone knew that was not so. We, therefore, gave up the pretense after two or three days. Jean and I found jobs within two weeks following our move to Chicago. Jean's job was as a secretary with a state agency. I found employment with Best Foods in Argo Ill. I remember, with some amusement, what happened when I was first hired with Best Foods. The company required new employees to take a test prior to being officially hired. Although I do not recall much about the contents or questions on the test, it didn't seem that difficult. After the scoring of the test was completed, I was led upstairs to the second floor. I immediately felt positive about my score on the test because all the heavy work was done on the first floor. As I entered the second floor, I noticed people with white lab coats doing what was apparently highly skilled work. "Aha, thinking to myself, I must have aced that test." We continued to the third floor. Again, I figured that I must have surpassed even my own expectations. After all, everyone knows that management and administrative types always reside on the top floor. I noticed, however, that there were no people on the third floor, only large stacks of bags and very large holes in the floor. My guide gave me a cutter, pointed to the stacks of bags, and said to me: "Take this cutter, cut and dump the contents in those bags into those holes." "Good thing that I aced the tests, saying to myself in a somewhat sarcastic mummer, otherwise I would have been outside loading boxcars." Loading boxcars were one of my next assignments with the company. Life's lesson here is that your physical location in an organization is not necessarily the same as your status in an organization. History is replete with pronouncements regarding the pitfalls associated with assuming that one's physical location is indicative of their influence or life-location. I made the mistake of thinking that working on the top floor was reflective of my position in the organization. Fortunately, I did not make the mistake of losing my self-worth because of the low-level function that I was assigned. In fact, it further motivated me to work harder in my educational pursuit.

Jean and I had a church wedding on December 2, 1961, in Detroit. Jean's sisters and girlfriends served as bridesmaids. Jean was beautiful, despite the swollen eye which was partly covered by her wedding [veil]. It seems that the night before our wedding, her stepfather and mother had an altercation. Jean, being the take-charge person that she was, stepped into the path of her step father's punches that was intended for her mother. I just knew that some people in the church figured that I was responsible for Jean's swollen face. Many years later, Jean and I would lament over the fact that her mother looked absolutely stunning with her smooth skin and unblemished face.

Jean and I went back to Chicago the next day following the wedding because we both were due back at our jobs. A month later, we found and moved into our own apartment on the Southside of Chicago. It was a one-room studio apartment with a Murphy bed and a kitchen that was about six by four feet. Still, it was our own place. Our first child, Lisa, was born two years later when Jean was of twenty and I was of twenty-four. By that time, we had moved into a much larger and nicer apartment in the Chatham section of Chicago.

Becoming a parent had a profound impact on my life. We, Jean and I, had produced a human being that looked like the both of us. She had Jean's skin color and body structure, and my eyes and hands. Fullers were known for small eyes and large hands. I was happy that my daughter looked more like her mother. After all, her mother, Jean, was a pretty woman, but she was also a strong woman.

The physical and emotional strength that Jean had proved time and time again. For example, Jean walked almost three blocks, each morning, with Lisa in her arms, to the nearest bus stop. It was not uncommon for her to have to wait for 15-20 minutes for the bus. Keeping in mind that she was holding a newborn baby and waiting in those dreadful Chicago winters. After jean dropped our new-born off at the baby sitter, she still had to walk another three blocks to her job. Jean never complained even once about having to get up so early and carry a new-born for blocks to catch a bus across town and then walk three blocks to her job, nor did she complain about being away from her family and living in a strange city. Looking back, I'm more convinced now, than ever, of the impact that she had on molding our daughter Lisa. She has the same toughness and attention to detail that Jean had. I have often told my friends that if I'm in a fight, I want two individuals with me. My 6-foot four-inch son, Eric, and my 5-foot six-inch daughter, Lisa. While Eric, would help me defeat my attackers, Lisa, would destroy them.

Chapter Ten

Graduate School and the Stress of Being the "Only Black"

I remember well the kidding I had to take from the guys I worked with at the plant. They would all stop at the bar after work to drink beer and discuss women, and sports. I seldom went with them because I was taking evening courses at the community college in the city. They kiddingly called me "Schoolboy." "Hey. Schoolboy," "man, why don't you give it up, don't you know you'll be 28 by the time you finish college! "Yes," I always replied, "but I'm going to be 28 in four years anyway, and I 'd rather be 28 with a college degree than 28 without one." They would all laugh, dismiss my reply with a wave of their hands, and continue drinking their beer, discussing women and sports. I often gave their reasoning some thought, after all, I too enjoyed drinking beer and discussing women, and sports with the guys, however, the fact that most of these guys had been meeting at the same bar for years, to drink beer, and discuss women and sports was not my idea of a good use of my time.

Two years later, we moved back to Detroit where I completed my undergraduate degree, after which, I returned to Chicago to visit with family. I figured that since I was back in Chicago, and had some time, after visiting with family, that I would go out to Argo in hopes of seeing the guys that I used to work with. I figured that the best opportunity to see the guys in one place would be the club where they usually went after work. Sure enough, when I walked into the bar, it looked the same as it did when I left the area two years ago. All the guys were there sitting at the same table, drinking beer, and talking about women and sports. In unison, they all shouted out "hey schoolboy, over here." They seemed to be as glad to see me as I was to see them. Of course, they all wanted to know what I was doing now. I told them that I had finished my degree and was working for the City of Detroit's anti-poverty program and working on my master's degree. "You still going to college schoolboy?"

We spent the next hour or two talking about women and sports. The next day, I returned to Detroit, where I continued working on my master's degree. Two years passed, and I again went back to Chicago to visit family. And, like before I drove out to Argo in hopes of seeing my buddies. Yes, they were all still there, with one exception. One of the older guys had died, but a younger guy was now a part of the group. To my surprise, the discussion had shifted from talking about women and sports to talk about sports and women. Nevertheless, they had the same question for me: "schoolboy, what are you doing now?" I explained to them that I now had my master's degree in clinical psychology and was working for the University of Michigan, and my job involved training government workers in ten states.

Three years passed before I returned to Chicago. I could say that I returned to visit with family, however, that would be an untruth. I wanted to see for myself if the same guys were meeting in the same bar, having the same discussions. I looked forward to answering their proverbial question, "schoolboy, what are you doing now?" I must admit that I was delighted to tell them that I now was Dr. Fuller with a Ph.D. in psychology and living in Atlanta, Georgia. I told them that I was a director with the school system, in charge of a lot of "stuff" and was president of the National Association of Black Psychologist. While I felt proud of my accomplishments, I felt sad to think that these friends and associates of mine had not grown a bit over the past ten or twelve years but were nevertheless happy in their complacency.

I also felt some sadness for not telling them about the challenges that I had to face and overcome in order to achieve the things that I shared with them. For example, I left out the fact that I was initially not accepted into the master's degree program at Oakland University because my grade point average was not high enough. I was more certain, however, that they would appreciate what I did to be accepted into the program on a Probationary basis. Here's what I did. I found an old yellow legal pad and a pencil, and I sent a hand-written letter to the President of the university. I explained to the President that I was a Black, former Marine from the inner city of Detroit, from a family of twelve brothers and sisters. I emphasized the point to him that I was not seeking any special consideration, but rather a chance to prove that I could if given the chance, prove that I could do masters' level college work. In about two weeks, I received a letter from the university admitting me into the master's Clinical Psychology Program on a probationary basis, further stating that I would have to maintain a minimum of a three-point average to remain in the program.

I vividly remember my first day at Oakland University. Entering my first class, I noticed that I was the only Black in the classroom. All the other students were upper-middle-class looking White students. This was not, however, what caused me some trepidation. All my educational experiences, from elementary, middle, and high school, were highly integrated, in addition, my three years in the Marine Corps involved living and working closely with White people. I, therefore felt no uneasiness being around them because they were white. Plainly put, it was the socioeconomic status of my classmates that raised some doubts for me.

Another factor that caused me some uncertainty was the feeling that most of the other students had some previous contact with the professor. They engaged in open conversations about events and activities that they had shared. I automatically assumed that they had already passed the course. After all, if you spend your leisure time fraternizing with the professor, it's only natural to glean some information about what he thinks is important relative to the course material. I must admit, however, that their apparent knowledge about the course subject was impressive. It did cause me to wonder if I was prepared to compete with them. What saved me was some of my previous experiences with whites. I noticed that they always had something to say that was, at least to some extent, related to the topic, regardless of its content. They also seemed to automatically place themselves in a superior position, relative to others, even though there was nothing that necessarily justified their assumed status. These cultural traits did not necessarily offend me, in truth, it was a kind of enjoyment observing them go through their predictable bull-shit.

I felt that they each knew that I was from the poor part of Detroit, and therefore, expected less from me as a graduate student. Although there were 15 students in the class, I felt like the "elephant in the room," there, but not really. In short, I received very little notice, even though I was the only Black in the room. I recall in one class session, we were discussing classical and operant conditioning. I added that several well-known psychologists, such as Skinner, Watson, and Pavlov, used various animals such as dogs and rats, to test their respective behavioral change theories. I casually mentioned that rats were probably the most difficult and problematic to use in an experiment because they were primarily nocturnal animals. All my classmates looked at me as if I had cursed the Pope. "You mean that you have actually seen a live rat?" One student asked. "Well, the rat wasn't actually alive, I replied, "it was dead in the rat-trap that I had sat in the kitchen the night before." Although I was surprised and taken aback by the attention given to me, I decided to seize the moment and expound on my comment. I went on to explain that in true psychological experimentation, the clinical environment must be as realistic as possible, otherwise, the results could be contaminated by extraneous variables, thereby increasing the likelihood of drawing inaccurate conclusions. In effect, since rats are nocturnal animals, their stimuli must be administered in their natural dark environment. "Take that, you sucker!" I screamed in silence, from that moment on, my input was "golden" to my university classmates. I finally found something that they didn't know anything about! They, of course, had no way of knowing that I had just read the information the night before. At that moment, I realized that my white counterparts were not necessarily smarter than me, they simply had read more stuff. Following that episode, I learned a valuable life-lesson: *good preparation is a prerequisite for good performance.*

To be completely fair, my initial experience with my white classmates in graduate school taught me several very important coping skills for functioning in a white educational environment. I begin to apply my learned racial coping skills upon entering my first class at Georgia State University in Atlanta. The first thing that the professor did was to explain to the class a brief, yet the current history of the university. This was, by the way, 1972. He recounted what the current president of the university had announced only two years earlier. According to the professor, the president said "no nigger will ever cross this universities' threshold." Remember, it was reported that the president of Georgia State University made this statement in 1968, not in 1938 or eighteen-sixty-eight, but in 1968 the year that Martin Luther King was assassinated. I must also note, at this point, that I, once again, was the only black in the room and in the doctoral program at Georgia State University. So, when the professor asked each student to introduce themselves, I while sitting in the very first row, something that I learned through my previous experience in an all-white situation, volunteered to go first. Facing the class, I said; *none of you in this class is equal to me. You cannot add anything, of value to my intellectual growth. You will gain from your involvement with me, but I will receive nothing of equal value in return,"* I then sat down.

As you might well imagine, silence fell over the room as stares of disbelief showed on the faces of my classmates. No one offered a rebuttal…the class continued. My intent was to set the bar high and establish the class hierarchy." Now, all I had to do was to walk-the-walk, since I had "talked-the-talk," or as we used to say in the hood: "Don't sell wolf tickets, if you can't bite anybody." The psychological premise that I was evoking is based upon a theory that I developed: *"You cannot create an original idea, while you are responding to something negative that someone says about you." In fact, "If you can predict someone's behavior, you can control his behavior."*

Chapter Eleven

113

Effie Fuller's "Baby Boy"-Taking a Stand

After I completed my master's degree, one of my former work associates with the War on Poverty program, Burt Bradley, told me that he was the Associate Director of a program ran by the University of Michigan and Ohio State University. Burt went on to inform me that there was an opening for someone with my background in working with urban communities and I should apply for the position. The fact that Burt was a liberal white guy from the Appalachian Mountains in Kentucky is only important contextually. I did apply and accepted the job with the program.

On the first day on the job, Burt set up a meeting for me to meet the program director, Joe Tuma. Joe was well into his sixties and had worked for years as a union boss in the Detroit auto industry. Joe welcomed me to the team and indicated that Burt had highly recommended me for the position. After a bit of small talk, Joe told me that the first task that he wanted me to perform was to go downstairs and wipe off some tables and bring them upstairs.

"Houston, we have a problem!" I looked at both Joe and Burt in disbelief. Surely, he must be kidding, I thought. Glancing at Burt, he too seemed shocked. I immediately replied that I did not accept the position to clean and carry tables! Joe Tuma seemed startled. It was obvious, that he had not been accustomed to having his commands rejected.

He suddenly moved back from the table and looked at Burt. Now, let me set both the context and rationale for my reaction. Less than two years prior, upon graduating from Michigan Lutheran College, where I received my bachelor's degree, I was offered the position of Dean of Admissions for the college, I turned that offer down because the City of Detroit had put me in charge of the War on Poverty training facility. In short, I was running my own training facility that included administrative and instructional staffs. Prior to that, I had been offered a management position with Sears, which I also turned down. So now, I've taken a position cleaning and carrying tables?

Hell no! Before the situation went completely sideways, Burt interceded and suggested that all staff should be involved since we had just moved into the building. That suggestion appeared to ease the tension and prevented me from walking out of the room with no job. *After all, I had already submitted the resignation of my previous job. But at that moment, none of that mattered to me, I was going to be "Effie Fuller's baby-boy," and stand up and speak up like a man, and that was that!*

Later that evening, while still perplexed about Joe Tuma's behavior, I gave some thought to why Joe Tuma would pull a stunt as he did, and it was a stunt. It didn't take me long to figure it out, Joe was trying to break my will by giving me a demeaning task to perform that would also serve as a reminder to the other staff members that he was in charge. That kind of action was consistent with what union bosses did to keep union workers in-check to ensure that they did not oppose paying dues and voting the way that the union bosses wanted them to vote. After my first meeting with Joe, our relationship changed for the better, I became Joe Tuma's favorite "go-to" guy for a couple of reasons. It took me only six months to establish myself as the most requested trainer throughout the ten states that the organization conducted sensitivity training. This fact was not lost on Joe Tuma. The other reason that Joe made me his "go-to" guy, was, in my opinion, the fact that I stood up to him, and showed no fear. Life's Lesson: *"Draw your line in the sand, but only after you know where the tide stops." And it is important to keep in mind, that the line that you draw in the sand is not only a barrier for the other person, it's a barrier for you as well.*

After the episode with Joe Tuma, Burt and I became even closer than before. We often did training sessions together for government organizations throughout the ten midwestern states. We made a good team…a white Kentuckian with an educated southern dialect and a black educated, street-wise, ex-marine from the east side of Detroit. Burt and I had different presentation styles. Burt's presentation was laid back, "folksy" and highly interactive. There seemed to be no structure, still, he was able to move the groups to a predetermined place. Even though Burt appeared unstructured, he was believable, you with a kind of feeling that he knew, what he was talking about. In short, the groups seemed to love his style. My style, on the other hand, was more structured and guided toward getting the point of the presentation across. But still, like with Burt, the groups seemed to like my style as well.

In retrospect, our presentation styles, like our personal styles, complemented each other. Burt was one of the most unprejudiced individuals that I have ever known. One could feel his genuineness when he talked about race. It is important to note that this was done in the late sixties, during the height of racial unrest, civil rights marches, and the burning of major sections of several urban cities. President Kennedy had been shot dead in Dallas, Malcolm X was assassinated in New York, Martin Luther King had been assassinated in Memphis, and James Brown had just released one of his biggest hits, I'm Black and I'm Proud. The purpose of the sensitivity training that Burt and I did was to close the racial division that existed throughout the nation, by dispelling the long-standing racial stereotypes. This was also during the time that blacks had big afros and wore dashikis and white males had long hair and facial hair. I laugh to myself when I think about a training session that Burt and I did in Minnesota.

The night before the training session, Burt washed his hair to give it an "afro" appearance. It worked; he indeed now had a very big "white-boy" afro. He proudly proclaimed that I too needed a bigger afro to make a lasting impression on the group. He suggested that I should wash my hair before the session to make my afro large. Attempting to control my laughter, I explained to Burt that black hair is different from white hair. When white people wash their hair, it expands, when black folks wash their hair, it draws up to the point that our brain is starved for oxygen. Burt had to acknowledge that he had missed that aspect of the "black experience" but would note it and incorporate it into his race sensitivity presentation.

The Life Lesson here is that there really are some differences between whites and blacks that are not offensive to either race. Differences, whether between people, places or the weather, are natural and wonderful. Unfortunately, the problem comes when we feel the need to attach values to the differences, rather than to value the differences.

Burt had developed a racial sensitivity presentation that he named the "Redford Study." The name, Redford Study, emanated from what was, at one time, a predominately white community (Redford Township) located on the outskirts of Detroit. The Redford Study was an exercise and simulation designed to dispel some of the negative stereotypes held by some whites about blacks. One of the historical stereotypes was that blacks are not as smart as whites, as suggested by some ability tests. The questions on the Redford Study were designed to demonstrate that mental ability or intelligence is to some extent, shaped by cultural and not innate mental ability. One of the questions asked in the study was "what is the proper way to cook greens?" Whites from northern cities always failed that question, for a couple of reasons. The primary reason was that most whites had no idea what "greens" were. Whites that thought that they were more enlightened thought that "greens" were the ingredients in a salad, and you, therefore, prepared greens by pouring your favorite dressing on the greens. Yes, the questions in the study were purposely designed to favor blacks, not whites. Still, the intended point was often made clear. That point was that much that is an intelligence test is based upon cultural and or regional factors. This point was not lost on me either, especially when, I made a visit to the Educational Testing Service (ETS) in Princeton New Jersey, where most of the ability and intelligence tests are written. I recall walking into the building where the actual writing takes place. There must have been at least 150 or more test writer sat individual desks, writing test items. After walking through the enormous space and observing the process, I was left with one overriding question, "Where are the black people?" I still don't know the answer to that question. I do know that I did not see a single person of color in that place, at that time, writing test items. While the point may seem trivial, it served to shape and guides my educational and career path throughout my professional and personal life. In effect, my master's degree was in clinical psychology or psychometrics, the science of measuring mental capacities, and I was currently working as an evaluation specialist. *My primary motivation, however, was even more personal. I felt that I not only had something to prove to myself but also for all those persons who had their lives negatively impacted by the results of a paper-pencil test.* One specific example that comes to mine was when Jean and I was looking through some old papers; we came across one of my last high school report cards. The summary of my years in high school was summed up by one counselor's assessment: "...Definitely not college material." Lucky for me that I already had my bachelor, master, and Ph.D. degrees before reading the counselor's prognoses. *"Life's Lesson: Never allow anyone else's negative assessment of your potential guide you."*

Chapter Twelve

Leaving Detroit for Atlanta

About a year after completing my master's degree, the Detroit initiative for the training program ended. Staff was, however, offered positions in other locations, mostly out of Detroit. But, his seven daughters and Mary Jo packed up his camper and moved to Atlanta. Several staff persons decided to get other jobs and remained in Detroit. Two weeks after Burt moved to the Atlanta project, he called me and suggested that I should consider relocating to the Atlanta project, because Atlanta was great, especially for blacks. As it would happen, I had previously visited Atlanta to bid on a training contract with Bell and Howell for my consulting company. It was during the month of May, the weather was spring-like and warm, dogwoods were in bloom, Hunter Street and underground Atlanta were alive.

The Atlanta University Center that was made up of a consortium of historically black colleges, including Atlanta University, Morehouse College, Spellman College, Clark College, and Morris Brown

College was inspiring and uplifting. In short, Atlanta had a lot going for it. The fact that I didn't get the contract with Bell and Howell did not change my positive impression of the city. After all, I was only bidding against a company headed up by Andy Young, who later became the Mayor for the City of Atlanta, and the United States Ambassador to the United Nations, and Maynard Jackson, who had just been elected as the first African American to serve as Mayor for the City of Atlanta.

Everything considered I believed the move to Atlanta was a good idea, for several reasons. Atlanta was a much better location than the other three locations available to me, which included New Jersey, Los Angeles, or Pontiac Michigan. In addition, Atlanta was going to pay me twenty thousand dollars a year and that was a good salary in 1970. I talked over it with Jean. Like always, she was fine with whatever I wanted to do, even though she was six months pregnant with our second child. So, once again, for the third time in nine years, Jean, myself, and our eight-year-old daughter, would be relocating to another state to make our home. Also, once again, Burt and I would be working together, this time, in Atlanta for Ohio State University with the local school system.

I moved to Atlanta two weeks in advance of Jean and Lisa to report at my new job and to find housing for the family. I stayed in the Holiday Inn in downtown Atlanta for the two weeks prior to relocating the entire family. I was both shocked and amused when I went down to the Holiday Inn restaurant for lunch to see the buffet containing greens, cornbread, and fried chicken. "Ok, then," I'm thinking to myself, "This might not be too bad!" That was the first surprise about Atlanta. The other surprise involved the work culture. At about nine o'clock each morning, all work stopped, and the entire building went to the cafeteria for breakfast, which was free. The third surprise was that before every meeting, two things happened, the building director told several "good old boy stories," after which we all prayed. Not surprising to those who knew me, a soon became proficient at telling "good old boy" stories, but not so well with the praying.

Jean was excited about moving to a new city and into a very nice neighborhood, and a very nice tri-level brick house. More importantly, Jean did not have to work, after all, she was six months pregnant with our second child, Eric. She seemed at peace with being a stay-at-home-mom. Still, I felt a little uncomfortable with the fact that we had no relatives in Atlanta and Jean did not know anyone in the city, but, overall, we were happy.

The next ten years passed quickly and involved several major changes in our lives. Eric, my son, was born that March, I completed my Ph.D., and was promoted several times. For some reasons, I became a much sorted after guest on TV and radio shows in the Atlanta area. Much of the interest in me came from the fact that I took controversial positions on most social issues. For example, on one television show, I presented most compelling arguments, as to why the Jews had no legal right to occupy some of the Palestinian lands in 1948 and declaring it to be a Jewish state. As you might imagine, I received a lot of flak from the Jewish community and my Jewish classmates at Georgia State University. In truth, I cared less about the Jewish and Palestinian conflict, I just knew that the one thing that you could not do, was to speak against the Jewish community without repercussions. Again, one of the coping strategies that I had picked up while being the "only black" in graduate school was to always have something to say about most things, whether you cared about the issue or not. For me, I was simply learning to cope and whenever possible, be in control of every situation. During that same period when I was gaining a lot of attention for being controversial, Burt asked me to stand in for him on his radio show for an entire week. I did, and again, as before, I acquired a sizable listening audience by engaging them in provocative topics with an edge. For example, I shared some of the research that suggested that there was an inverse relationship between having sex and life expectancy. In short, the more you "do it" the sooner you die. The more recent and credible research indicates just the opposite relationship between sexual activity and life expectancy.

Some of my more standard and professional involvement with the media concerned social and political topics. Julian Bond, who helped to establish the Student Nonviolent Coordinating Committee (SNCC) and was chairman of the National Association for the Advancement of Colored People, and I discussed the impact of poverty and education upon black progress in the twentieth century on his hour-long radio show. Strangely enough, I did not feel "out of my league" discussing these topics with him, after all, he and I were about the same age, I was thirty-seven, he was thirty-six. Although, clearly, his experience and background were much superior to mine, still, *I made it a point to not only prepare well but feel comfortable enough in all situations to hold my own.* My one-on-one with

Coretta Scott King, although less intellectual, was more challenging out of deference to Dr. Martin Luther King, her famous husband. Mrs. King, and I, were discussing some contractual arrangements between the King Center and the Atlanta Public School System. *One could tell that Mrs. King knew that she had power and standing, and she did not let anyone forget that, not in a mean way, but rather in a "matter-of-fact" way.*

Chapter Thirteen

Confronting Racism and Myself

Following my tenth year in Atlanta, I longed for the times that I had spent meeting with my friends after work. We were all college grads working in professional type jobs in the downtown section of Detroit. We would all gather at Foster's in the downtown area near the Detroit River where we would have drinks, make passes at the ladies that we knew that we would not or could not follow up on, talked sports, and go home to our wives. It was a good outlet, we all knew each other, and as the old TV sitcom "Cheers," "everybody knows your name." Some of us had "street" names. My "street" name was "Demon;" there was Ron, who answered to "Silver Fox," and Carl, called affectionately, "Rev." I got my street name from my best friend Harold, who one day heard my mother referring to my brother as a "demon." So, Harold started calling me "little demon" he later dropped the little, and from that day forward, I was called "The Demon." Ron, better known as the "Silver Fox," although the youngest in the group, was prematurely graying, so silver fox made sense. Carl, the Rev, always entered the lounge citing a passage from the Bible: *"For the grace of God has appeared, bringing salvation for all people* [Titus 2:11] **[1],** was his favorite. But to quote a phrase from one of my all-time favorite movies: [Forest Gump] *"Life is like a box of chocolates…you never know what you're going to get."* 1 *Case-in-point, Ron, the Silver Fox, is currently the pastor in one of the largest churches in the city of Detroit. Carl, the Rev, is a practicing lawyer in Detroit.*

Jean, while being a homemaker and mother to two young children, completed her bachelor's and master's degrees. And, as if that was not enough, we had our first home built. I can't help but laugh when I think of the time when Eric was about four years old; he brought his friend to the house bleeding. He proudly announced that he told his friend that his daddy was a doctor and could stop the bleeding from his head. I explained that "daddy" was not that kind of doctor and we should take his friend home right away.

Eric seemed to understand and accept my explanation for taking his friend home. Years later, when Eric was ten years old, it was more difficult and painful for me to attempt to explain racism and slavery to him. In fact, I cannot recall a more difficult task as a parent for multiple reasons. First and foremost, neither Eric nor my daughter Lisa had ever experienced racism. Both had lived in mixed communities and interacted with people of different races. It would be both naïve and disingenuous for me to assert, that racism did not exist in some of those mixed communities, however, overt racism is generally not as pronounced in middle and upper-middle-class communities as in lower socioeconomic areas. In retrospect, part of my difficulty in explaining racism to my son had something to do with the fact that too, even at 33 years of age, had not resolved all my issues with racism. One classic example of the psychological scars of racism was the fact that I had difficulty watching black individuals of families, on television or in movies, showing affection for each other. It took a lot of self-analysis to resolve the cognitive dissonance caused by watching blacks show affection toward other blacks. *"In psychology, cognitive dissonance is the mental stress or discomfort experienced by an individual who holds two or more contradictory beliefs, ideas, or values at the same time."*

The conflicting beliefs that I and other blacks experience watching blacks showing affection while complex, is historically associated with slavery and more recently with the media's portrayal of blacks. It was not so long ago that the only images of blacks on TV or in movies were performing subservient functions or as slaves. The showing of affection between individuals or groups was reserved for whites only, not blacks. As a result, when blacks view other blacks showing affection, it is a contradiction between what they have been conditioned to expect and what they are seeing. Let me be clear, whites are equally conflicted, when they see blacks demonstrating affection toward one another. In effect, there is a symbiotic relationship between what blacks expect of themselves and what whites expect from blacks. Simply put, blacks are impacted negatively internally and externally. My intent here is to show that no one is left unscarred where racial hatred and racial divisions can persist. *The same cognitive dissonance that causes some blacks not to feel comfortable when they see blacks exhibiting affection toward other blacks, is the same conflict experienced by some whites when they see whites treating blacks with hate and disdain.* This dissonance may also cause some individuals to allow skin color to override their sense of right and wrong. I was a part of and observed one real-life example. I was training a group of prison guards at Jackson State Penitentiary in Michigan. The group of guards was from both racial groups, i.e., blacks and whites. One of the guards seemed especially bigoted, expressing clear racial sentiments. Many of the other white guards seemed to agree with his views on race. I asked the guard what his background was. He told the group that he was a sniper for Germany during the 2nd World War. I then asked the group, how they felt about the fact that they agreed with a person that had hidden in trees and shot their fathers, grandfathers, and other relatives, and that others like him had marched hundreds into ovens to be burned. On the other hand, I explained, the blacks that some of you despise, were brought to the country in chains, worked the lands for nothing, and fought in all the wars and returned home to be told that they could not sit at a lunch counter and order a hamburger because of the color of his skin. Nevertheless, you prefer the former Nazi sniper over the blacks.

You might be wondering, at this point, why I have focused so much of my writings on race. While that is a good and obvious question, the answer is more complicated and thought-provoking. Remember, this book is about how one's view of the world and life, is impacted and guided by our perceptions and experiences as children and adults. That is, moving from childhood to adulthood is a journey, albeit more psychological and social, it is nevertheless a journey. *How can a black individual in America not have his or her perception, and search for identity and not be affected by racism?*

Chapter Fourteen

Confronting Racism in Institutions

It becomes essential to remember that the soul, however you define it, is the repository of all experiences. Some of these experiences cause both psychological and practical damage to the individual. One example, that will forever be a corner in my soul, happened in 1991 and involved my wife, who was employed at Georgia Tech. The headlines of The Atlanta Inquirer, a black Atlanta newspaper, [Vol. 30, No.33] was the following: *"Discrimination Charged to Georgia Tech."* The newspaper article went on to explain how that African American employees at Georgia Tech had filled an anti-discrimination suit against Georgia Tech based upon irrefutable evidence. Included in the evidence was the following;

(a) African American employees held only 1% of administrative or faculty positions.

(b) White PhDs. were paid 27% more than African Americans working in similar positions with comparable seniority or experience as Whites.

(c) Whites holding bachelor's degrees receive an average salary of $50,036 per year, compared to $29, 534 per year for African Americans.

(d) African Americans filing discrimination grievances often faced retaliatory and punitive actions, which brings us to my wife's situation.

The short version is this, as reported by The Atlanta Inquirer: "Dr. Jean Fuller, who is described as the epitome of professionalism, has a Doctorate Degree in Higher Administration and Policy Setting. In 1987 she won the Outstanding Researcher of the Year award and has passed with honors every job evaluation criterion imposed upon her…the only African American in the department. She had ten years of seniority which was longer than anyone in the department. She was told that the department was going to be restructured and she would no longer be working at Georgia Tech, although, no other employee would be affected by the reported restructuring," *Once again, Effie Fuller's "baby boy" drawing upon many of signs from life's journey, went into action. In short, we, my wife, and a host of others, including various members of the civil rights community, brought Georgia Tech to its proverbial knees.* I will always remember the Thursday morning, down of Auburn Ave., the president of Georgia Tech, and several of his associates, met with me, Dr. Joe Lowery, of the Southern Christian Leadership Conference (SCLC), Joe Beasley, of the Rain Bow Coalition, the NAACP, and Reverend Tim McDonald, President of the Concerned Black Clergy, to address Georgia Tech's treatment of African Americans. More specifically, the meeting was about the plan to fire my wife, Jean, on the following Monday.

I had learned, over the years of being the "only black in the room," to always be prepared with data. I had also developed my own strategy of only carrying only a limited number of papers that contained the data. After introductions and I was asked to present the case against Georgia Tech, I distributed one sheet of paper containing the data to each person at the table. The data on the single sheet of paper that I distributed was the same data that I had gathered and given to the local newspapers in the city. I said nothing for a "pregnant-moment," Dr. Crecine, President of Georgia Tech, was the first to speak: When I first heard about Dr. Fuller's case, referring to my wife Jean, I thought that something was wrong about it. He then asked me if I would agree to meet with him in his office. During the meeting in his office, Dr. Crecine told me that Jean's position would be restored and in fact, she would be receiving an increase of $11,000 in her new position. He also asked me if I knew who was directly responsible for my wife's situation. Something inside of me said that I should not tell him about the role that Dr. Norman Johnson, the only black in his administration, had played. It had been reported that he had said that, not only should Jean be fired, she should lose all of her accursed vacation time.

As we, Tim McDonald and I walked out of Dr. Crecine's office, we passed Dr. Norman Johnson, entering the office, and he had a very strange, "sheepish" look on his face. Tim McDonald, who knew the role that Dr. Johnson had played at Georgia Tech relative to black employees, said to me, "You should have burned that sucker!" I replied that we might be able to use him at some later point. *I was guided by what Machiavelli, in the "prince:" said: "You should never wound an animal and send him into the forest because he will be waiting there for you while he heals from his wounds," [2]* What does all of this have to do with life's journey's signs? Everything.

Therefore, my long answer to a short question is the following. As with a broken bone, the first thing that happens is a callus or bump forms where the break occurs. The body deposits calcium to the injured part of the bone and makes it stronger at least during the healing process. We already know that the body acts in a similar way to most damaged areas of the human body. Why would damage to the black person's psychic be any different? Black people in

America have been damaged through slavery, racial discrimination, and social bigotry. Following the healing process of the body, a bump forms (callus) at the psychic level, following our example, the psychic-bump is manifested through self-hate or lack of self-worth, as have been demonstrated throughout the history of black people in America. During the biological healing process, calcium is deposited at the damaged area. The calcium, for purposes of our thesis, is represented by avoidance, denial, in order to allow the healing process to take place. As it has often said, a broken bone, once healed, is stronger than before it was initially broken. Although there is no scientific evidence to support this dissertation, the logic holds promise.

Following the logic that has been presented in the previous section, understanding, how and why the subject of race, for black people in general, and for black males like myself, is so important. Our entire existence has and continues to be permeated by our racial experiences, both collectively and individually. For example, my wife and I went to a family reunion on my mother's side of the family in Tennessee. One of the family members had the actual chair that my great grandmother sat in while she was being sold as a slave when she was nine years old. The plantation owner that bought her, fathered seven children by her. One of those seven children was my mother's mother. Although I could not bring myself to sit in the chair, I could almost feel the nine-year-old heart beating in fear. Knowing that aspect of my history will forever be a part of my soul and my heart. I now pose a question for the reader: *"Will my damaged and broken heart and soul heal like a broken bone and repair itself, thereby making me stronger?"*

Chapter Fifteen

Reading the Signs on the Journey to the soul

The movement from childhood to adulthood is a journey to the soul. On the way to the soul, the journey presents many things to guide us. Sometimes, during the journey, we don't see what we're looking at. Like a well-constructed highway, the journey provides signs to assist in completing our journey, like what direction we are heading in, how fast we should be moving, and how far the next exit is. Well, planned highways also give us various things to watch out for; detour ahead, congestion, or a soft shoulder. I, like most people, have seen these various signs along my journey to my soul, as a man.

Looking backward, I can recall several "highway" type signs that helped to shape, as well as guide me in my journey from childhood to my soul as a man. I now pose a short question for the reader: "Will my damaged heart and soul now be stronger?"

On one lazy summer day, while sitting on my patio, I noticed an ant, pulling something that must have been more than twice its size. The ant would pull the object about 5 or 6 inches, drop the object, and move 10 or 12 inches in the direction that it was initially headed. The ant would then go back to the object and continue to pull it to the location that it had just inspected. The ant would continue this process until it reached its destination. From the eyes of a child, it appears that the ant could benefit- from having more ants to help it pull the object. But, from the perspective of a man seeking to find his soul, the perception was different. *"How brilliant," I thought. Even an ant has sense enough to look ahead to see if there are any obstacles in its path.* If only we humans would follow that simple procedure, just think of the pitfalls that we could avoid. Observing ants provided me with yet another example of guidelines while seeking to find one's soul as a man. Have you ever destroyed an ant mound? If you stayed around long enough, you would observe that the ants would immediately begin to rebuild the mound, even while you were still in the process of destroying it. From the eyes of a child, the ants were not methodically going about the task of rebuilding, they were instead, frighten and disorganized. *However, the man, in search of the best route to his soul, would conclude that unlike some humans, the ant did not give up, curse the mound destroyer, turn on its mound mates, or find another mound to occupy.* In short, the road to the soul is not always paved and smooth. There may be bumps, and potholes, as well as bad travelers and unreadable highway signs. The highway to the soul does not necessarily follow a straight line. There may be detours, roadblocks, and bad weather; therefore, we must learn to stay focused.

Chapter Sixteen

Losing Jean

The loss of individual who were close to us impacts each of us differently to some degree. From the eyes of a child, the person died, simply went away, and will return at some point. As we mature through childhood, the impact of our lost diminishes, and in time, we forget. As adults, however, we are not spared the hurt and anguish associated with losing those close to us. Like other life experiences, the impact may not always be at the conscious level, still, we are changed, to some degree.

Although it has now been more than four years since Jean died, it seems like yesterday to me. And yes, I have been impacted. In fact, it is more accurate to say that I am not the same person that I was before Jean died. Her death has softened me in some respects, while in other respects, I have hardened. While I have become more introspective, in that I now have a greater appreciation of the little things in life, I have become less tolerant of small things, made to seem important.

Jean died on November 26, 2014. The death certificate listed cardiac arrest and active coronary syndrome as the cause of death. Jean had sarcoidosis. *Sarcoidosis is an inflammatory disease that affects multiple organs in the body, but mostly the lungs and lymph glands.* Although the research indicates that sarcoidosis is not inherited, Jean's full sister and their father suffered from and died from sarcoidosis. Although she probably had the condition early on as a child, consistent with the research, it did not become evident, until she was in her late thirties or early forties. I notice Jean's shortness of breath after we moved to Atlanta, although, at the time, it did not appear to pose a problem for her. Although Jean had no problem going to the doctor, and she went often, the specific cause of her shortness of breath was not diagnosed until we moved into our new house that had three levels, with the master bedroom located on the upper level.

I had a stair lift installed to going up to the second floor. The stair lift seemed to make Jean's life better. She was no longer restricted to either floor. Still, though, Jean's condition appeared to deteriorate. I not only began to take Jean to our doctor, at her request but also, I went into the examination room with her to see the doctor. Her reasoning was that I could better understand what the doctor was saying. On one evening, Jean appeared to be having more difficulty than normal breathing. I insisted on taking her to the hospital. The hospital conducted several tests and concluded that she could return home. Upon returning home, Jean sat down by the desk in the kitchen area. I turned on the fireplace in the other room and asked her if she wanted to join me there. She indicated that she just wanted to sit at the desk before going to bed. I thought that strange because Jean seemed to enjoy sitting with me by the fire and just talking. At about 2 am that night, I heard Jean calling me." Chest!" "Chest" I jumped out of bed, almost in a panic, searching for her. I went to the bathroom area, she was not there. I then went to the stairway. Jean was lying face-down on a carpet, but not moving. She was not conscious. I called her and turned her over. Her entire body was limp. I immediately called 911. They instructed me on administering CPR on her, which I did for several minutes until the emergency unit arrived. The emergency staff told me to leave the area while they attempted to resuscitate her. I followed the ambulance to the hospital, where I stayed until Jean passed. The night before Jean died, I told the nurse, when I was going to go home to change clothes, the nurse told me that that was not a good idea since Jean had a "rough" night and that I should say close. The nurse further informed me that they were declaring a "code blue," and I should go to the waiting area and wait for further instructions. While in the waiting area, I told my daughter what was happening and that it did not look good. When the nurse called me back to the room, I noticed that there was five or six medical staff treating Jean. The nurse pulled me aside and told me that although they had revived Jean and she was breathing with the help of the machine, it would not last long. The nurse further told me that I would have to make a decision if Jean stopped breathing again. The decision, she explained was whether I wanted them to resuscitate Jean again or let her go peacefully, but in either case, Jean would never be the same, because the brain had gone too long without oxygen. I told her not to resuscitate Jean again. As the nurse had predicted, Jean's breathing stopped again, and she was gone. At that moment, and I don't know why I remembered what Jean had said to me just a few days ago. In Jean's words: whenever there were problems, that seemed to have no answer, you always found a way." This time, "I could not find a way."

How do I carry on without her? There is an emptiness inside of me that I cannot fill. I still hold on to the thought that her death is nothing but a bad dream, and I will wake up and everything will be as it was. Jean will be sleeping beside me. I will watch her sleep for a while. I'll get up, shower, and head downstairs to make my coffee and read the morning paper. In a while, I'll go back upstairs to the bedroom. Jean will sit up in the bed when she hears me coming. I'll sit on her side of the bed facing her, and we will talk. She seems to especially enjoy our morning talks, and that pleases me because it pleases her. But this is not a dream. Jean is not sleeping next to me. There's just an empty space where she used to sleep. How do I carry on without her? I must think about what to do next. I'm like a ship lost at sea without a map or a rudder. It comes to me that Jean was my map and my rudder. How do I carry on without her? Falling back into my dream state, I hear Jean upstairs moving the chair under her vanity, where she will sit for nearly an hour applying her makeup with the care and skill of a surgeon. Later, I'll listen for the first sound of her stair lift as she descends to the kitchen. She'll have breakfast consisting of skim milk and cereal. She has all her makeup on as if she is on her way to the mall. Everything about her appearance is perfect. Her nails appear freshly painted and help to accentuate her diamond wedding ring. I watch her every move. I can see her looking to see if I'm watching her. She seems pleased when she knows that I'm watching her. That pleases me because it pleases her. How do I carry on without her?

During the time that I am alone, which is most of the time, I attempt to look within myself to see if there was anything that I could have done differently to save her life. Should I have insisted that she spend another night in the hospital? Should I have stayed up with her into the night? The last word that she spoke was my name. She called out to me in a voice filled with desperation. I've placed the large picture of her in her walk-in closet. I go there each morning to share with her my thoughts, concerns, and to tell her how much I love and miss her. The look in her eyes gives me assurance that she knows that I will handle things. She once told me that I always found a way to make things right when there seemed to be little hope. These words always stayed with me whenever I thought that I could not find a solution to whatever. How can I carry on without her?

I look forward to my morning talk with her, even though the talk is only to her picture. Still, it gives me comfort to bear all that resides in my mind and my heart. The look in her eyes seems to travel throughout my entire body. I feel her presence in my soul. She speaks to me in the reflections in her eyes. Funny, I never realized how beautiful her eyes are. How do I carry on without her? My days are often filled with self-pity, internal tears, and convenient distractions. I cannot allow myself to linger in the catatonic state that thinking about her causes me. She would expect me to do better and act differently. She would expect me to carry on without her. Still, I often find myself unable to move beyond the moment. When my life-long friend, lover, wife, advisor, and mother of my son and daughter died, part of my soul died with her, the best part of my soul. Still, Jean is no longer with me; how do I carry on without her?

It has now been four years since Jean died, it seems like yesterday. To some extent, I'm still in a mental fog. *My days are measured and filled with superfluous activities. I still feel the anger associated with what I feel is "life's unfairness," My interest in forming new relationships with women, is, for the most part, nonexistent. I am also more conscious of my own mortality.*

Jean and I took a total of five consecutive cruises together. We both loved cruises, they were for both of us, a chance to just be together with no one except the two of us to focus on. So, it is understandable that four years after Jean's death, that I would want to take a cruise to reminisce about our times together. Only this time, there would be no Jean, just me and the memories. Yet, it seemed like a good idea and would give me a chance to catch up on the writing of this book and to experience part of the Cuban culture. The goal of catching up on the book writing, not so much. However, the opportunity to observe and learn about aspects of the

Cuban culture, especially race relations, seemed to be a good replacement for not catching up on the book. In addition, the opportunity to learn about how Cubans view the perceptions of the journey to the soul, presented too much to miss.

On the third day of my Cuba cruise, while sitting on the top deck back of the ship, one of the waiters stopped by to ask how I was doing and was I having a good day. Although he looked to be no more than 18 or 19, I later learned that he was twenty-five and was from Indonesia and his name was Aman. I felt the need to allow Ha'mond to do most of the talking because he initiated the conversation and seemed to have the need to ventilate. Conversely, I sensed the need within myself to indulge him because he seemed to be seeking someone to listen and to share his pain. Aman agonizingly told me that he hated the ship and had made several requests to be transferred back home to Indonesia to be with his wife for only a month who was expecting their child. As I listened intently, I tried to push away the feeling that he probably would not survive the remaining seven months of his eighth-month contract. In an attempt provide whatever solace I could, I told him how great he would feel to know that he and his wife had produced another human being that would probably look like a combination of both, and that alone was worth the wait. Aman nodded in agreement and further said that just talking about it makes him feel better.

Although my brief encounter with Aman did not give me much information about Cuban culture, after all, he was from Indonesia, it did, however, give me a peek into his journey toward finding his soul. Although much of his pain appeared to be associated with making the transition from being a single man to a newly married adult, the experience of wanting to be with his wife, and son to be a child, was shaping and refining his soul.

My next encounter with a person on the ship worked in the ship's gym. His name was Oda, he was from South Africa, but lived in the Bahamas. Unlike Aman, Oda was not married, and generally enjoyed his job on the ship. He talked at length about issues in his native country of South Africa. He indicated that he left the country because he did not see the opportunity for growth economically and did not want to put in the two years of mandatory military service. He further indicated that his goals as a child had changed as he entered young adulthood. It appears that Oda is well on his way to reaching the soul level of being a man.

The life lesson in this instance was a reminder that human pain does not discriminate based on age, gender, nationality, or race. It is not bound by language differences or even the edicts of different Gods. It simply is what it is and resides in the hearts and souls of us all.

Like all good stories, this story too has a happy ending. As the cruise ship docked at the Port of Miami, and passengers and crew members were disembarking, I saw Ha'mond leaving the ship, carrying his duffel bag. He was smiling and waving goodbye to his shipmates. I felt certain that Ha'mond's request to be released from his contractual obligations, had been granted, and he was heading home to Indonesia to be with his wife, and soon to be a child. *In short, he had found his soul.*

EPILOGUE

As human beings, we seek affirmation of self. In effect, the universal question of "Who am I?" is always a part of our life-long search. When we are children, the "who am I" question is nonexistent, because the child thinks that nothing else of importance exists, except for the "I" person. As we mature, we begin to realize that most of the things that we want depend, to a large extent, upon pleasing or appeasing others. The extent to which we are willing to go, or put another way, the extent to which we are willing to give of our "personhood" for the purpose of getting what we desire, helps to form and shape, the self and define the soul.

It is a universal concept and belief that as children, we make decisions and choices that are not driven by either experience or knowledge. What is less discussed, or acknowledged, is that even though children, of course, do not have a great reservoir of either experience or knowledge to draw upon for making decisions or choices. Nevertheless, the decisions and choices that they make still impacts the forming of the soul.

By now, after reading this text, I am certain that you understand that for me, the soul is the composite of everything we encounter in our individual lives. You must also realize that the soul is never a "passive" entity in the process of defining either our humanity or our actions. I end this book with a statement from the eyes of a child (my granddaughter, Erica), to her younger sister, Macy: **"Macy: You are born, you get old, and then you die, let's play! "Indeed."**

A summary of what was learned while traveling along the highway of life

The soul is the composite of everything we encounter in our individual lives. The soul is never a "passive" entity in the process of defining either our humanity or our actions.

[Matthew 16:26] Jesus asks what good is it for a man to gain the whole world but lose his soul.

While the answer that Erica gave to Macy, was a sufficient enough answer to satisfy her inquiry, it also helped to bring a harsh, yet, true reality to mind for me, namely. While the soul may be eternal, Living is terminal.

From the eyes of a child, I saw a big place, filled with images and faces of things and people that I knew, and felt safe with. From those same child's eyes, I saw and believed that everything I saw was about me and for me. My mother, father, and sisters and brothers were there just for me, and that was good, and the way that it should have been, from the eyes of a child. This was my new world, and at six, I felt more than able to cope with it. Let's play!

Our mothers and fathers were referred to by their first names and the children got pats on our heads like pets. In my lighter moments, I figured that they were, in their own way, attempting to be friendly. Still, the feelings of hurt were ever present.

These were the only times that the sisters were heard speaking to each other in their native polish tongue. "ci ludzie są szaleni I leniwi," translation: {These people are crazy and lazy}.

The folds of crisp blue-white snow did melt and turn to slush, Christmas passed, toys broke, and I turned seven down on Hastings Street, where the unspoken rules made sense, unforeseen events were predictable, yet surprising, and even strangers were known and welcomed down on Hastings Street.

The "life-Lesson" learned here was never dated an angel with no wings. "Wing" is a metaphor for reputation or deeds. Unfortunately, in many cases, we have no idea about a person's reputation or deeds. As a result, we generally only have isolated observations or "feelings" to guide us, and, when you think about it, "feelings" are pretty good indicators of character or "Wings."

The first was a piece of advice, as a very young child, living in Detroit. "Boy doesn't touch that hot stove!" I did, and still have the scars to prove that the stove was hot.

"Self-hate" has been and remains an issue among black people. It is in fact, likely one of the main factors impacting our journey from childhood to adulthood.

I did notice, however, that the older I got, the more I noticed that women who were about something, were more drawn to "ideal, serious type men than to the flashy, fast-talkers type.

None of you in this class is my equal. You cannot add anything of value to my intellectual growth. You will gain from your involvement with me, but I will receive nothing of equal value in return,"

I was going to be "Effie Fuller's baby-boy," and stand up and speak up like a man, and that was that! "Draw your line in the sand, but only after you know where the tide stops," And it is important to keep in mind, that the line that you draw in the sand is not only a barrier for the others, it's a barrier for you as well.

My primary motivation, however, was even more personal. I felt that I not only had something to prove to myself but also for all those persons who had their lives negatively impacted by the results of a paper-pencil test.

Never allow anyone else's negative assessment of your potential guide you.

I made it a point to not only prepare well but feel comfortable enough in all situations to hold my own.

One could tell that Ms. King knew that she had power and standing, and she did not let anyone forget that, not in a mean way, but rather in a "matter-of-fact" way.

There really are some differences between whites and blacks that are not offensive to either race.

The same cognitive dissonance that causes some blacks not to feel comfortable when they see blacks exhibiting affection toward other blacks, is the same conflict experienced by some whites when they see whites treating blacks with hate and disdain.

Draw your line in the sand, but only after you know where the tide stops," And it is important to keep in mind, that the line that you draw in the sand is not only a barrier for others, it's a barrier for you as well.

You cannot create an original idea, while you are responding to something negative that someone says about you."
If you can predict someone's behavior, you can control their behavior.

I still feel the anger associated with losing Jean and "life's unfairness," ... I am also more conscious of my own mortality.

How brilliant" I thought. Even an ant has sense enough to look ahead to see if there are any obstacles in its path before proceeding.
However, the man, in search of the best route to his soul, would conclude that unlike some humans, the ant did not give up, curse the mound destroyer, turn on its mound mates, or find another mound to occupy.

I was guided by what Machiavelli, in the "Prince" said: "You should never wound an animal and send him into the forest because he will be waiting there for you while he heals from his wounds,"

While the soul maybe everlasting, Living is terminal.

"You are born, you get old, and then you die, let's play!" Indeed!

Footnotes

[1]. Scripture quotations are taken from the *Holy Bible,* New Living Translation, copyright ©1996, 2004, 2007. Used by permission of Tyndale House Publishers, Inc., Carol Stream, Illinois 60188. All Rights Reserved.

[2]. Machiavelli, N. (2017). *The Prince*. [online] www.gutenberg.org [Accessed 18 Jul. 2017].